Kids  LOVE Indiana

Your Family Travel Guide to Exploring Kid Friendly Indiana! 500 Fun Stops & Unique Spots

Michele Darrall Zavatsky

Dedicated to the Families of Indiana

For the latest major updates corresponding to the pages in this book visit our website:

www.KidsLoveTravel.com

Although the authors have exhaustively researched all sources to ensure accuracy and completeness of the information contained in this book, we assume no responsibility for errors, inaccuracies, omissions or any other inconsistency herein. Any slights against any entries or organizations are unintentional.

- ❏ **_REMEMBER_**: *Museum exhibits change frequently. Check the site's website before you visit to note any changes. Also, HOURS and ADMISSIONS are subject to change at the owner's discretion. If you are tight on time or money, check the attraction's website or call before you visit.*

- ❏ **_INTERNET PRECAUTION_**: *All websites mentioned in KIDS LOVE INDIANA have been checked for appropriate content. However, due to the fast-changing nature of the Internet, we strongly urge parents to preview any recommended sites and to always supervise their children when on-line.*

- ❏ **_EDUCATORS_**: *There are suggestions for finding FREE lessons plans embedded in many listings as helpful notes for educators.*

KIDS ♥ INDIANA ™ Kids Love Publications

TABLE OF CONTENTS

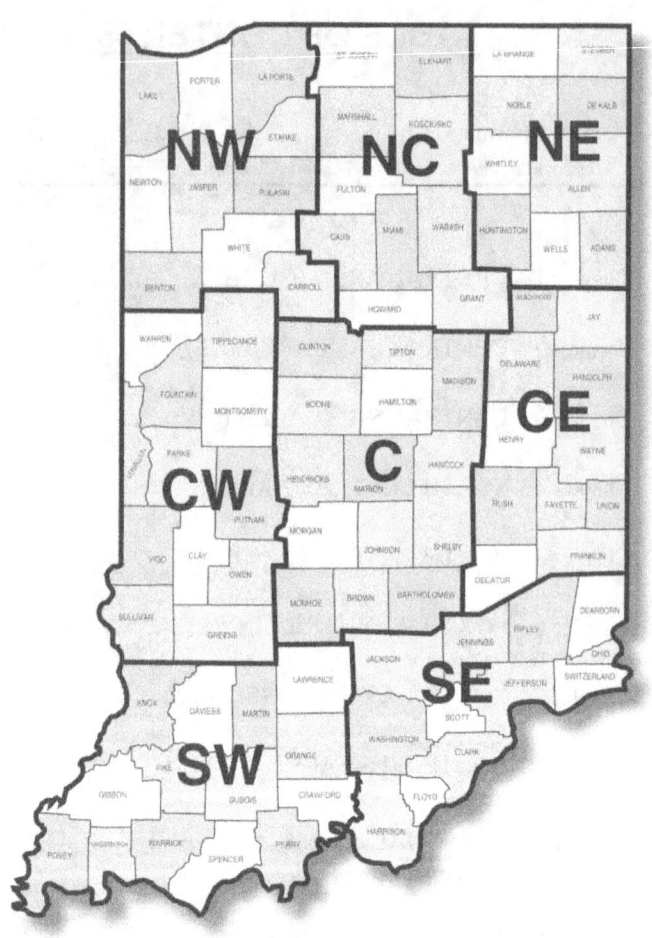

Chapter Area Map

State Map

(With Major Routes and Cities Marked)

HOW TO USE THIS BOOK

(Some hints to make your adventures run smoothly)

BEFORE YOU LEAVE:

Each chapter represents a two-hour radius area of the state or a Day Trip. The chapter begins with an introduction and Quick Tour of favorites within the chapter. The listings are by City and then alphabetical by name, numeric by zip code. Each listing has tons of important details (pricing, hours, website, etc.) and a review noting the most engaging aspects of the place. Our popular Activity Index in back is helpful if you want to focus on a particular type of attraction (i.e. History, Tours, Outdoor Exploring, Animals & Farms, etc.).

Begin by assigning each family member a different colored highlighter (for example: Daniel gets blue, Jenny gets pink, Mommy gets yellow and Daddy gets green). At your leisure, begin to read each review and put a highlighter "check" mark next to the sites that most interest each family member or highlight the features you most want to see. Now, when you go to plan a quick trip - or a long van ride - you can easily choose different stops in one day to please everyone.

Know directions and parking. Use a GPS system or print off directions from websites.

Most attractions are closed major holidays unless noted.

When children are in tow, it is better to make your lodging reservations ahead of time. Every time we've tried to "wing it", we've always ended up at a place that was overpriced, in an unsafe area, or not super clean. We've never been satisfied when we didn't make a reservation ahead of time.

If you have a large family, or are traveling with extended family or friends, most places offer group discounts. Check out the company's website for details.

For the latest critical updates corresponding to the pages in this book, visit our website: www.kidslovetravel.com Click on *Updates*.

ON THE ROAD:

Consider the child's age before you stop at an exit. Some attractions and restaurants, even hotels, are too formal for young ones or not enough of an adventure for teens. Read our trusted reviews first.

Estimate the duration of the trip and how many stops you can afford to make. From our experience, it is best to stop every two hours to stretch your legs or eat/snack or maybe visit an inexpensive attraction.

Bring along travel books and games for "quiet time" in the van.   (see tested   travel products on www.kidslovetravel.com) As an added bonus, these "enriching" games also stimulate conversation - you may get to know your family better and create memorable life lessons

In between meals, we offer the family snacks like: pretzels, whole grain chips, nuts, water bottles, bite-size (dark) chocolates, grapes and apples. None of these are messy and all are healthy.

Plan picnics along the way. Many Historical sites and State Parks are scattered along the highway. Allow time for a rest stop or a scenic byway to take advantage of these free picnic facilities.

WHEN YOU GET HOME:

Make a family "treasure chest". Decorate a big box or use an old popcorn tin. Store memorabilia from fun outings, journals, pictures, brochures and souvenirs. Once a year, look through the "treasure chest" and reminisce."

WAYS TO SAVE MONEY:

Memberships - many children's museums, science centers, zoos and aquariums are members of associations that provide FREE or Discounted reciprocity to other such museums across the country. AAA Auto Club cards offer discounts to many of the activities and hotels in this book. If grandparents are along for the ride, they can use their AARP card and get discounts. Be sure to carry your member cards with you as proof to receive the discounts.

Supermarket Customer Cards - national and local supermarkets often offer good discounted tickets to major attractions in the area.

Internet Hotel Reservations - if you're traveling with kids, don't take the risk of being spontaneous with lodging. Make reservations ahead of time. We don't use non-refundable, deep discount hotel "scouting" websites (ex. Hotwire) unless we're traveling on business - just adults. You can't cancel your reservation, or change them, and you can't be guaranteed the type of room you want (ex. non-smoking, two beds). Instead, stick with a national hotel chain you trust and join their rewards program (ex. Choice Privileges) to accumulate points towards FREE night stays.

State Travel Centers - as you enter a new state, their welcome centers offer many current promotions.

Hotel Lobbies - often have a display of discount coupons to area shops and restaurants. When you check in, ask the clerk for discount pizza coupons they may have at the front desk.

Attraction Online Coupons - check the websites listed with each review for possible printable coupons or discounted online tickets good towards the attraction.

GENERAL INFORMATION

ATHLETICS

- ❑ **C** – Bloomington. Indiana University Athletics. (866) IUSPORTS or **www.iuhoosiers.com**.
- ❑ **C** – Indianapolis Tennis Center. IUPUI Campus. (317) 278-2100. RCA Championships. US Tennis Association training site.
- ❑ **C** – Indianapolis. The Natatorium. Indiana University, 901 West New York Street. (317) 274-3517. Three indoor pools of national and international aquatic events.
- ❑ **CE** – Lafayette. Purdue University Athletics. (765) 494-3197 or (800) 575-0285 or **www.purduesports.com**
- ❑ **CE** – Muncie, Ball State University. (765) 285-1474. Mid-American Conference Division I-A. **www.ballstatesports.com**
- ❑ **NC** – University of Notre Dame. (574) 631-3000 or **https://fightingirish.com/**

CAMPING

- ❑ Hoosier Camper Guide. (800) 837-7842 or **www.campindiana.org**

CANOEING

- ❑ Liveries listings. **www.indianaoutfitters.com**

FISH HATCHERY - STATE RUN

- ❑ **Statewide**
- ❑ Telephone Number: (317) 232-4080. Division of Fish and Wildlife. **https://www.in.gov/dnr/**
- ❑ Hours: Monday - Friday, 8:00am-4:00pm
- ❑ Admission: Free
- ❑ Tours: By appointment
- ❑ Note: Sites are Driftwood (Area SE), Avoca (Area SW), Cikana (Area C), Fawn River (Area NE), Twin Branch (Area NC), Mix Sawbah (Area NW), and Bass Lake (Area NW).

State run outdoor fish farms produce 200,000 to 1 million fish each year per site. Any of the six farms might raise trout, large mouth bass, blue gill, sunfish, and black crappie for stocking state parks. The caretakers usually start the tour with a slide show. Then, it's out to the ponds.

You'll be informed about the proper soil and depth of each pond and the vegetation that is most wanted. At the Avoca site, they have more than enough spring water from a cave nearby to supply their thirteen ponds. The best time to visit is harvest time when they drain the pond down to a minimum pool and wade through the water with a sieve to collect fish. In summer and early winter, the rainbow trout are easiest to see as they jump to the surface when you feed them.

HIKING
- Get Out & Go Guide. Tourism Division. (317) 232-4070. **https://www.in.gov/dnr/state-parks/recreation/trails/**

RECREATION
- Indiana Recreation Guide. Department of Natural Resources. **https://www.in.gov/dnr/publications-and-maps/indiana-recreation-guide/**

SNOWMOBILING
- Indiana Snowmobile Association Hotline (574) 679-4006 **www.indianasnowmobilers.com**

STATE PARKS / RESERVOIRS
- (317) 232-4124 or **https://www.in.gov/dnr/state-parks/**

TOURISM
- Indiana Tourism **https://www.visitindiana.com/**
- C - Indianapolis Tourism (800) 958-INDY. **https://www.visitindy.com/**
- NE - Fort Wayne/Allen County CVB – Visitors Center, 1021 South Calhoun **www.visitfortwayne.com**.

Check out these businesses / services in your area for tour ideas:

ANIMAL SHELTERS - Great for the would-be pet owner. Not only will you see many cats and dogs available for adoption, but also a guide will show you the clinic and explain the needs of a pet. Be prepared to have the children "fall in love" with one of the animals while they are there!

BANKS - Take a "behind the scenes" look at automated teller machines, bank vaults and drive-thru window chutes. You may want to take this tour and then open a savings account for your child.

CITY HALLS - Halls of Fame, City Council Chambers & Meeting Room, Mayor's Office and famous statues.

ELECTRIC COMPANY / POWER PLANTS - Modern science has created many ways to generate electricity today, but what really goes on with the "flip of a switch". Because coal can be dirty, wear old, comfortable clothes. Coal furnaces heat water, which produces steam that propels turbines, that drives generators that make electricity.

FIRE STATIONS - Many Open Houses in October, Fire Prevention Month. Take a look into the life of the firefighters servicing your area and try on their gear. See where they hang out, sleep and eat. Hop aboard a real-life fire engine truck and learn fire safety too.

HOSPITALS - Some Children's Hospitals offer pre-surgery and general tours.

NEWSPAPERS - You'll be amazed at all the new technology. See monster printers and robotics. See samples in the layout department and maybe try to put together your own page. After seeing a newspaper made, most companies give you a free copy (dated that day) as your souvenir. National Newspaper Week is in October.

PETCO - Various stores. Contact each store manager to see if they participate. The *FUR, FEATHERS & FINS*™ program allows children to learn about the characteristics and habitats of fish, reptiles, birds, and small animals. At your local *PETCO*, lessons in science, math and geography come to life through this hands-on field trip. As students develop a respect for animals, they will also develop a greater sense of responsibility.

PIZZA HUT & PAPA JOHN'S - Participating locations. Telephone the store manager. Best days are Monday, Tuesday and Wednesday mid-afternoon. Minimum of 10 people. Small charge per person. All children love pizza – especially when they can create their own! As the children tour the kitchen, they learn how to make a pizza, bake it, and then eat it. The admission charge generally includes lots of creatively made pizzas, beverage and coloring book.

KRISPY KREME DONUTS - Participating locations. Get an "inside look" and learn the techniques that make these donuts some of our favorites! Watch the dough being made in "giant" mixers, being formed into donuts and taking a "trip" through the fryer. Seeing them being iced and topped with colorful sprinkles is always a favorite with the kids. Contact your local store manager. They prefer Monday or Tuesday. Free.

SUPERMARKETS - Kids are fascinated to go behind the scenes of the same store where Mom and Dad shop. Usually you will see them grind meat, walk into large freezer rooms, watch cakes and bread bake and receive free samples along the way. Maybe you'll even get to pet a live lobster!

TV / RADIO STATIONS - Studios, newsrooms, Fox kids clubs. Why do weathermen never wear blue/green clothes on TV? What makes a "DJ's" voice sound so deep and smooth?

WATER TREATMENT PLANTS - A giant science experiment! You can watch seven stages of water treatment. The favorite is usually the wall of bright buttons flashing as workers monitor the different processes.

U.S. MAIN POST OFFICES - Did you know Ben Franklin was the first Postmaster General (over 200 years ago)? Most interesting is the high-speed automated mail processing equipment. Learn how to address envelopes so they will be sent quicker (there are secrets). To make your tour more interesting, have your children write a letter to themselves and address it with colorful markers. Mail it earlier that day and they will stay interested trying to locate their letter in all the high-speed machinery.

MISSION STATEMENT

At first glance, you may think that this is a book that just lists hundreds of places to travel. While it is true that we've invested thousands of hours of exhaustive research to prepare this travel resource...just listing places to travel is <u>not</u> the mission statement of these projects.

As a child, I was able to travel throughout the United States. I consider these family times some of the greatest memories I cherish today. Quite frankly, I felt that most children had this opportunity to travel with their family as we did. However, as we started our own family, we found that this wasn't necessarily the case. We continually heard friends express several concerns when deciding how to spend "quality" and "quantity" family time. 1) What to do? 2) Where to do it? 3) How much will it cost? 4) How do I know that my kids will enjoy it?

Interestingly enough, as I compare experiences with my family, many of our fondest memories were not made at an expensive attraction, but rather when it was least expected.

It is my belief and mission statement that if you as a family will study and <u>use</u> the contained information <u>to create family memories</u>, these memories will grow more well-rounded children. Our ultimate mission statement is, that your kids will develop a love and a passion for quality family experiences that they can pass to another generation of family travelers.

We thank you for purchasing this book, and we hope to see you on the road (*and hear your travel stories!*) God bless your journeys and Happy Exploring!

Happy
Exploring,
Michele

Chapter 1
Central Area - (C)

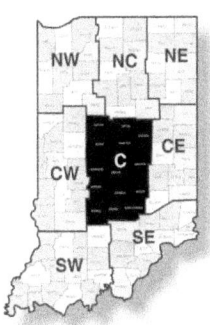

2

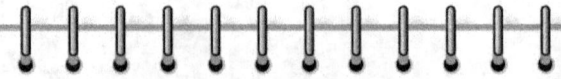

Our Favorites...

* Mathers' Museum - Bloomington
* Mayberry Cafe - Danville
* Connor Prairie - Fishers
* James Whitcomb Riley Old Home - Greenfield
* Indiana Museum - Indianapolis
* Indianapolis Children's Museum - Indianapolis
* Indianapolis Motor Speedway - Indianapolis
* Indianapolis Zoo - Indianapolis

Future Indy Racing Legend!

ANDERSON FINE ARTS CENTER

32 West 10th Street

Anderson 46015

❑ Phone: (765) 649-1248, www.andersonart.org
❑ Hours: Wednesday-Friday Noon-5:00pm, Saturday 10:00am-5:00pm, Sundays 2:00-5:00pm. Open at 10:00am on Saturdays.
❑ Admission: $3.00 adult.
❑ Tours: Passport to Adventure group tour is $3.00 per person.

The lower level houses a children's hands-on gallery, display areas for temporary exhibitions of student and community art, and a classroom. The Passport to Adventure Tour is of the Arts Center's permanent hands-on gallery for children ages four to twelve. Learn about color, texture, line and form while creating artworks and reproducing famous paintings such as the Mona Lisa and Arrangement in Gray and Black (ex. Whistler's Mother). Included in the ten activity stations are color mixing, spin art, sculptural puzzles, texture rubbings, and a silhouette booth.

ANDERSON SPEEDWAY

1311 Pendleton Avenue

Anderson 46016

❑ Phone: (765) 642-0206
   www.andersonspeedway.com
❑ Hours: Fridays Race at 7:30pm (May-August), Saturdays Race at 8:00pm (April-October).

Historic Anderson Speedway is home to weekly racing along with the annual Little 500 Sprint Car Race and the 400-Kendall Late Models. Admission usually $18.00 adults, $7.00 children.

ANDERSON SYMPHONY

Paramount Theatre, 1124 Meridian Street

Anderson 46016

❏   Phone: (765) 644-2111 or (888) 644-9490
     www.andersonsymphony.org
❏   Admission: $20.00-$41.00 adult, $13.00-$25.00 child.
❏   FREEBIES: Games & Activities
     http://andersonsymphony.org/symphony-for-kids-games-
     activities/

The recognized Anderson Symphony Orchestra, surrounded by the majestic Moorish architecture, intimate atmosphere and fine acoustics of the circa 1929 theatre make this a grand way to conduct an evening. For kids are concerts with Halloween and Christmas themes and the Youth Orchestra. The Historic theatre has playings of the old theatre organ.

MOUNDS STATE PARK

4306 Mounds Road (I-69 to CR 320 to CR 232)

Anderson 46017

❏   Phone: (765) 642-6627 http://in.gov/dnr/parklake/2977.htm
❏   Admission: $7.00-$9.00 per vehicle.
❏   Educators: http://in.gov/dnr/parklake/files/sp-
     Mounds_TeacherPrepPuzzles.pdf

The park features 10 distinct "earthworks" built by a group of prehistoric Indians known as the Adena-Hopewell people. The largest earthwork, the "Great Mound", is believed to have been constructed around 160 BC. It's a circular enclosure almost ¼ mile in circumference. Stand in the middle and catch the feeling of Ancient tribal ceremonies that might have been held. The nature center is located in the Bronnenberg House (open April-October 9am-4pm), built from materials in the surrounding woods. Bridle Trails, Swimming / Pool.

MONROE LAKE STATE RESERVOIR

4850 South SR 446

Bloomington 47401

❑ Phone: (812) 837-9546   www.in.gov/dnr/parklake/2954.htm
❑ Admission: $7.00-$9.00 per vehicle.

Scenic bluffs, rolling hills and lushly wooded areas surround Monroe Lake. Also features a Nature Center and Volleyball Courts, Boating, Camping, Fishing / Ice Fishing, Fourwinds Resort and Marina, Hiking Trails, Boat Rentals, and Swimming / 2 Beaches.

WONDERLAB

308 West Fourth Street (3 blocks west of the bus depot)

Bloomington 47404

❑ Phone: (812) 337-1337,   www.wonderlab.org
❑ Hours: Tuesday, Wednesday & Thursday 9:00am-6:00pm, Friday-Saturday 9:00am-5:00pm, Sunday 1:00-5:00pm.
❑ Admission: $14.50 (age 1+). Military discounts.
❑ Notes: Nature Pack – interactive activity sheets, guides and experiments.

The Lab provides kid-friendly science experiments like Bubble-Airium, How Things Work, Discovery Garden (live animal habitats, cave, tree house and WaterWorks), and Natural Science (Southern IN fossil dig, saltwater aquarium). Each month WonderLab focuses on a different area of science, health and technology. Hands-on activities associated with the program theme change throughout the month. Check the calendar for special guest scientist programs.

INDIANA UNIVERSITY

530 East Kirkwood Avenue, Suite 104
(IU Visitor Information Center)

Bloomington 47408

- ❑ Phone: (812) 856-GOIU, **https://admissions.indiana.edu/visit/**
- ❑ Tours: Sunday early afternoon campus tours. Self-guided tours - https://visitorcenter.indiana.edu/doc/iub_campus_walking_tour.pdf
- ❑ Notes: Stop by the Indiana Memorial Union (largest student union in the country) for a snack or shop in the bookstore. See separate listing for Mathers Museum located on campus. Tours and many buildings closed during school breaks.

Some attractions include:

- ❑ **MEMORIAL STADIUM / ATHLETIC COMPLEX** (1001 East 17th Street, 812-855-9618 Stadium). The building houses the IU Department of Intercollegiate Athletics and is the home of the "Hoosiers". Of special interest are the trophy cases in the lobbies, the Athletic Hall of Fame, and the Olympic and NCAA , which hang in the arena. The public is welcome to tour the facilities between the hours of 8:00am-5:00pm, Monday-Friday. Please check-in with the receptionist at the football office complex (east stands).
- ❑ **LABORATORY OF ARCHAEOLOGY** (423 North Fess Street at Ninth Street, 812-855-9544) . A major study and research facility in the field of Hoosier Archaeology. Included in the lab is a public museum devoted to Great Lakes/Ohio Valley archaeology and ethno-history. Hours: Tuesday-Friday 9:00am-4:30pm, Weekends, see exhibit through Mathers Museum. Free.
- ❑ **HILLTOP GARDEN AND NATURE CENTER** (2301 East Tenth Street). Access is the entrance drive to Tulip Tree Apartments off 10th Street. Home to one of America's oldest youth gardening programs, established in 1948. Greenhouses, ponds and perennials. Call for hours.

For updates, visit our website: www.KidsLoveTravel.com

❑ ART MUSEUM/LILLY LIBRARY (Fine Arts Plaza, East
Seventh Street, 812-855-5445). Ranked among the nation's
best university art museums, the IU Art Museum holds
more than 35,000 objects including paintings by such
artists as Picasso and Monet. Artworks of the Western
World from Byzantine to modern times, Asian and Ancient
art, the art of Africa and the Pacific and the Pre-Columbian
Americas are all at the museum. The building was
designed by the world-renowned architectural firm, I.M.
Pei and Partners. Hours: Tuesday-Saturday 10:00am-
5:00pm, Sunday Noon-5:00pm. Free.

❑ GREENHOUSE (East Third Street, 812-855-7717).
Located next to the I.U. Biology Department building, the
Jordan Hall Greenhouse lets you stroll through green
gardens, flowers and tropical jungles. It is a thriving
greenhouse of unusual, exotic plants from every corner of
the world. Individuals may tour during regular business
hours. Group tours are available by appointment. Hours:
Monday-Friday 8:00am-4:00pm, Saturday & Sunday
9:00am-3:00pm. Free.

❑ KIRKWOOD OBSERVATORY (Dunn Woods -East of
Indiana Avenue, near Fourth Street). Built in 1900, the
facility contains a 12-inch refractor telescope and other
astronomical equipment. Viewing is available every clear
Wednesday night when classes are in session.

MUSEUM OF ARCHAEOLOGY AND ANTHROPOLOGY (FORMALLY MATHERS MUSEUM)

416 North Indiana Avenue (Northwest side of Indiana University)

University Campus), **Bloomington** 47408

- ❏ Phone: (812) 855-MUSE
  https://iumaa.iu.edu/index.html
- ❏ Hours: Tuesday-Friday 9:00am-4:30pm, Saturday-Sunday 1:00-4:30pm. Closed during semester breaks.
- ❏ Admission: FREE. Metered and IU Permit parking is available at the McCalla School parking lot on the corner of Ninth Street and Indiana Avenue. Parking is available on surrounding streets during the weekend.
- ❏ Tours: Recommended. Guides bring the interactive displays to life. Call to schedule.
- ❏ Notes: Gift shop with items as low as $1.00. We'd recommend that each child purchase a different, unusual musical instrument to form a cultural band when they get home.

Want to take a trip around the world? This Museum has exhibits, events, and educational programs that give you a chance to learn more about objects from Brazil to Zambia... 20,000 artifacts from across the world reveal traditions, values and beliefs in objects people create and use every day. One key focus of the new Museum is Native American people of the American Midwest, including artifacts from Angel Mounds near Evansville. The kids hands-on area has pretend houses in a European Village where you can dress up and play house from different cultures. Check out "Dancing the Ancestors: Carnival in South America" and "World Music: Themes and Variations".

After learning about their huge ethnic instrument collection (our favorite part), ask the guide for assistance in making one of your own using recycled everyday materials. Unusual and exciting exhibits engage children here!

For updates, visit our website: www.KidsLoveTravel.com

MONROE COUNTY HISTORICAL MUSEUM
202 East Sixth Street (6th and Washington Sts.)

Bloomington 47408

❑ Phone: (812) 332-2517 www.monroehistory.org
❑ Hours: Tuesday-Saturday 10:00am-4:00pm.
❑ Admission: $1.00-$2.00 (age 6+).

In the old, historic Carnegie Library, the giant limestone pot gives you a visible landmark from the Washington Street entrance. "See Stories, Touch Time, Make Memories" is their motto. Permanent Exhibits focus on the worker, education, entertainment, pioneers, and transportation in Monroe County. Many exhibits are set up as walk-up "rooms" of history with genuine artifacts from that era including the Circus era.

BLOOMINGTON SPEEDWAY
5185 South Fairfax Road (3 miles south of town to Old SR 37 South, east at stop light on Fairfax Rd)

Bloomington 47426

❑ Phone: (812) 824-7400 www.bloomingtonspeedway.com
❑ Hours: Generally every Friday (mid-April-Sept). Pit Gate open 4:30pm, Grandstand open 5:30pm, Laps 6:30pm, Racing 7:30pm.
❑ Admission: Average $20, more for special events. Children 12 and under are FREE. The fastest quarter mile dirt oval track for sprint, modified and street stocks.

CARMEL SYMPHONY ORCHESTRA
1 Carter Green, **Carmel** 46032

❑ Phone: (317) 844-9717.
www.carmelsymphony.org
❑ Season: (September-May). Some outdoor performances summer.
❑ Admission: Average $10.00-$15.00.

Family concerts. Enjoy quality musical performances by talented local artists.

BARTHOLOMEW COUNTY HISTORICAL SOCIETY MUSEUM

524 Third Street, **Columbus** 47201

❑   Phone: (812) 372-3541
       www.bartholomewhistory.org
❑   Hours: Tuesday-Thursday 10:00am-4:00pm.
❑   Admission: Free.

The museum is housed in the McEwen-Samuels-Marr home built in 1864. Permanent exhibits include a period bedroom and parlor and a pioneer exhibit from the early 1800's. "The Train Goes Through Town - Columbus, 1886," is an HO Scale Model Train Display of downtown Columbus in the 1886 era. Also featured are hands-on activity areas.

KIDSCOMMONS CHILDREN'S MUSEUM

300 Washington Street (& 4th, The Commons Mall)

Columbus 47201

❑   Phone: (812) 378-3046, www.kidscommons.org
❑   Hours: Tuesday- Saturday 10:00am-1:00pm and 2:00-5:00pm,
       Sunday 2:00-5:00pm
❑   Admission: $9.00 (age 18 months-99). Children must be
       accompanied by caregiver.
❑   Notes: Large indoor children's playground in the mall.

The programs here are especially for children 2 to 12 emphasizing science, the visual arts, and community happenings. Activities vary monthly and might include an art-making station where kids may paint, create sculptures or self-portraits, or make inventions with "scrap" material from local industries. Investigate the science of optics on the laser harp or recreate human movement using a robotic arm. Toddlers may gravitate to the tunnels, building blocks and a soap bubble station where kids can see how big a bubble they can create and explore why they burst.

ZAHARAKO'S CONFECTIONARY

329 Washington Street (off I-65, downtown, across the street from
Commons Mall)

Columbus 47201

❑   Phone: (812) 378-1900 or http://zaharakos.com/
❑   Hours: Tuesday-Sunday 11am- 9:00pm.

A Columbus landmark and a "must-see" for kids is located
downtown. Popular from the day it opened on October 20,
1900, The Greeks, or Zaharako's Confectionery as it is
known today, was founded by three brothers from Greece.
At the time, it was common for settlers from abroad to
become shopkeepers. "Zaharaoplastion" is Greek for
Confectionery. Zaharako's is known for its turn-of-the-
century decor; a self-playing, German pipe organ installed in
1908; two onyx soda fountains (once on display at the St.
Louis World's Fair) installed in 1905; Christmas decorations;
and the GOM Sandwich – sloppy joe, grilled, Hot Fudge
Sundae, and other menu items. Fun names like "Fireball",
"Double Up" or "Double Down" are called out with many
orders.

HENDRICKS COUNTY HISTORICAL MUSEUM

170 South Washington, **Danville** 46122

❑   Phone: (765) 745-9617 https://hendrickscountymuseum.org/
❑   Hours: Friday & Saturday 11:00am-3:00pm. (closed Jan/Feb)
❑   Admission: Donations accepted.

Located in the former sheriff's residence and jail (1866-
1974). Visit and have your picture taken in "jailbird" attire.
Also, see items relating to domestic life, agriculture, military
history and education.

CONNER PRAIRIE

13400 Allisonville Road (NE of Indianapolis, I-465, exit 35
or I-69, exit 5)

Fishers 46038

❑ Phone: (317) 776-6006 or (800) 966-1836
www.connerprairie.org

❑ Hours: Tuesday-Sunday 10am-5:00pm (April-October),
Thursday-Sunday 10:00am-5:00pm (November-March). The
outdoor grounds are closed November - March . The indoor
experience areas, including Discovery Station, Create.Connect
and Craft Corner are open year round. Waterplay area open
summers only. EST

❑ Admission: $25.00 adult, $22.00 senior (65+), $19.00 child (2-
12). $8 admission for all (November-March).

❑ Note: 1823 William Conner House is a restored settler's and
statesman's home - the finest in town. Tours every 20 minutes for
$1.50 additional charge. Museum Center exhibits, gift shop and
Persimmons Restaurant (lunch/dinner). Programs range from an
1836 wedding to the dark uncertainty of the Underground
Railroad.

Unlike many other historical villages in the Midwest, when
you enter Prairietown, you really do interact as if you've
been transported in time! All of the townspeople dress and
act their character according to the year 1836. Mention of
modern conveniences like pagers and cell phones is
responded to with a blank stare. Your initial conversations
may be a little awkward but you get the feel of things
quickly.

Pretend you're staying the night at the Golden Eagle Inn (for
12 ½ cents!) and then walk through town to visit neighbors
like the Quaker printer, Jeremiah Hudson, or the Fentons
(weavers - you can purchase yarn dyed naturally), or the
Campbells (Dr. and Mrs. - definitely upper class).

The kids' favorites were the baby lambs just born in the
Conner Barn and the Schoolhouse. Sit on split log benches

For updates, visit our website: www.KidsLoveTravel.com

as the school master gives you lessons teaching the "loud" school method. Youngsters recite their different lessons aloud. Repetition is the key to learning and a ruler is used to discipline (not used on your first day of school, of course). Allow enough time to spend with chores like candle dipping, washing clothes on a washboard, spinning, gardening or by playing with 19th century toys in the yard.

Indoors, kids 9 and under like Discovery Station. Whether climbing the forest-themed play area, dressing up like a favorite critter, or building a puzzle, this is the perfect place for families, all year long. Or Craft Corner: Try your hand at take-home crafts. Here, you can try things like soap making, using an antique printing press, decorating a quilt square, or weaving.

JAMES WHITCOMB RILEY OLD HOME AND MUSEUM

528 Lockerbie Street (I-70 to SR 9 to US 40, Lockerbie Square)

Greenfield 46140

❏   Phone: (317) 462-8539

     https://rileymuseumhome.org/

❏   Hours: Thursday-Saturday 10:00am-4:00pm (April to October).

❏   Admission: $10.00 adult, $1.00 child (7-17).

❏   Tours: Every half hour, by reservation online.

Mr. Riley was born in Greenfield in 1849 and his 1044 poems brought him the name, Hoosier Poet. (They are mostly about Indiana and kids). Famous characters he developed were the Raggedy Man and Little Orphan Annie from people he talked with and observed, or, events like the circus in town or a harvest festival.

The best parts of the tour are the winding, creaky staircase, the rafter room, a cubby-hole and the chimney flue. Each spot plays a part in one of Riley's ghost stories. Little Orphan Annie used to tell stories that always ended "Er the Gobble-uns'll get you-ef you don't watch out!". Guides recite story poems throughout the tour - it was a delightful way to add mystique to a very simple home.

PRESIDENT BENJAMIN HARRISON HOME

1230 North Delaware Street (just north off I-65)

Indianapolis 46202

- ❑ Phone: (317) 631-1888
  www.presidentbenjaminharrison.org
- ❑ The museum is closed all major holidays, 500 Race Day, and the first three weeks in January.
- ❑ Admission: $16 adult, $15 senior/military, $11 student (5-17).
- ❑ Tours: guided tours every two hours Monday through Thursday 10am- 2pm, Fridays on the hour 10am-2pm, Saturdays on the hour 10am-3pm and Sundays on the hour from 12pm-3pm.
- ❑ Educators: Activities-craft & cartoon: http://www.presidentbenjaminharrison.org/visit/student-tours/activities-and-teaching-guides

See the 16 room Italianate Victorian home of the lawyer nominated for 23rd presidency in 1888. Harrison actually campaigned from his front porch and his daughter loved to sneak and slide down the three-story spiral staircase. Stand on the front stoop where Benjamin Harrison gave 80 "front porch" speeches to 300,000 people who came by to listen. In the master bedroom is displayed an old-fashioned home gym with weighted pulleys made from beautiful wood (a 19th century NordicTrack!) See the Library where election returns were tallied by telegraph. View a piece of Haviland White House china that Caroline Harrison designed choosing corn to surround the border.

Actual belongings of the Harrisons include an inaugural Bible, White House Tea Set and Parlor Sofa – but don't touch! Look for several unusual, specially designed, chairs Harrison loved.

ATOMIC BOWL / ACTION BOWL

1105 Prospect (I-70 exit 83A or I-65 exit 111/Fletcher, turn right, turn left on Virginia Ave)

Indianapolis 46203

❏ Phone: (317) 686-6006

❏ www.fountainsquareindy.com

❏ Hours: Tuesday-Thursday 1:00pm-9:00pm, Friday 1:00pm-midnight, Saturday 11:00am-Midnight, Sunday 1:00-7:00pm.

❏ Admission: $40.00 per hour per lane (up to 6 can bowl one lane). Includes free shoe rental.

The Fountain Diner is the biggest diner we've ever visited – bring the whole gang along. Definitely try their shakes, floats and a grilled chili dog.

Two Duckpin Bowling Alleys each represent a different period of time. Action Bowl is on the 4th floor and has been restored to the original time period of the building: the 1930's. Atomic Bowl is on the basement level and has been restored to the 1950's era. The Atomic features two juke boxes that play 45's with songs from the period.

There's also a Soda Fountain serving hand-dipped shakes, malts, root beer floats, and ice cream sodas. Duckpin bowling is very kid-friendly. The balls are just a little larger than softballs and are easily handled, even by toddlers. The duckpin bowling is so fun and silly, skill isn't really an issue.

EITELJORG MUSEUM OF AMERICAN INDIAN AND WESTERN ART

500 West Washington Street (White River State Park)

Indianapolis 46204

❏ Phone: (317) 636-9378, www.eiteljorg.org

❏ Hours: Monday-Saturday 10:00am-5:00pm, Sunday Noon-5:00pm.

❏ Admission: $20.00 adult, $16.00 senior (65+), $12.00 child (5-17) and full-time students w/ID.

❏ Tours: Daily 1:00 pm.

The Eiteljorg Museum is unique, one of two museums east of the Mississippi with both Native American and Western art. Contemporary artists who tell the story of today's West are represented and the Native American collection includes pottery, basketry, sculpture and other artifacts from all 10 North American native cultural areas. Western Family Discovery Area: Kid's Indian crafts or demonstrations offered. Five Diverse Stories of the West including totem poles, a mexican café, a cattle ranch, and the Eiteljorg's popular stagecoach and wagon-wheel activity. Pick up the Family Guide listing of activities. You'll feel you walked into a Santa Fe courtyard as you tour the rooms.

INDIANA STATE HISTORY CENTER

White River State Park Museum Complex (between Hall of Champions and Eiteljorg Museum)

Indianapolis 46204

❏ Phone: (317) 232-1637, www.indianahistory.org
❏ Hours: Tuesday-Saturday 10am-5pm. Sunday Noon-5pm.
❏ Admission: $15.00 adult, $14.00 senior (60+), $5.00 child (5-17).
❏ Notes: Gift shop with many Indiana-made items. Café.
  Educators: Curriculum guides (many unusual topics not seen elsewhere) https://indianahistory.org/education/education-resources/educator-resources/

The INDIANA EXPERIENCE: You Are There, which features three-dimensionally reconstructed historic photographs that include first-person interpreters, allowing visitors to step into another era.

Allowing visitors to travel through time using innovative technology, Destination Indiana is IHS's newest experience. You can now swipe, pinch and tap your way through more than 300 journeys including stories about African-Americans, the Civil War, the Ohio River, mapping the state, social justice and reform, rail transportation and agriculture.

The History Lab is a hands-on demonstration lab. Within

For updates, visit our website: www.KidsLoveTravel.com

that space, INvestigation Stations allow visitors to "do" history as they analyze historic documents, research family trees, search for clues in photographs and explore careers in history. Many "touch me", "listen to me" and especially "smell" stations(!) add to the living history.

INDIANA PACERS

125 Pennsylvania Street (Conseco Fieldhouse)

Indianapolis 46204

❏   Phone: (317) 917-2100, www.nba.com/pacers/

NBA Basketball. Boomer, the Panther is the fun team mascot and there's a fan club and kids pages/games on the website.

INDIANA SOLDIERS' AND SAILORS' MONUMENT/ COLONEL ELI LILLY CIVIL WAR MUSEUM

(Monument Circle - Meridian Street, Center of Town... You can't miss it!)

Indianapolis 46204

❏   Phone: (317) 232-7615
    www.in.gov/iwm/2335.htm
❏   Hours: Monument - Friday-Sunday 10:30am-5:30pm. Museum – Wednesday-Sunday 9:00am-5:00pm
❏   Admission: FREE. Observation Elevator: $3.00
❏   Tours: Observation deck open mid-April to mid-October.
❏   Note: The USS Indianapolis Memorial, five blocks west, is of historical significance also.

Challenge your energetic kids to the 331 stair climb to the glass-enclosed balcony at the top for a panoramic view. (An elevator is available up to the last 31 stairs). See many bronze and limestone carvings (enormous and detailed) of famous Indianans like James Riley and President Harrison. The largest sculptures are of Civil Wartime Scenes. Throughout the year, the monument's steps play to performers, politicians and festivals.

Indiana War Museum (continued)

Inside the base is a museum with interesting city and war insights telling the personal stories of Hoosiers who fought to protect the Union and supported the Civil War effort.

"Miss Indiana" tops the landmark with curved steps North and South and fountains with reflecting pools to the East and West.

INDIANA STATE CAPITOL BUILDING

200 West Washington Street (corner of Capitol Ave. and Washington St)

Indianapolis 46204

- ❏   Contact: www.in.gov/idoa/2430.htm
- ❏   Hours: Monday-Friday 8am - 5pm, excluding holidays.
- ❏   Admission: FREE
- ❏   Tours: Tours of the State House every weekday from 9am-3pm, excluding holidays. Weekend tours are offered Saturday at 10:15am, 11:00am, 12:00pm and 1:00pm. You must enter at the North door. Self-guided tour booklets are always available at the Information Desk or in Room 220.

Built in 1882 (on the site of the 1835 State House) with Indiana limestone, the building contains executive, legislative, and judicial offices. There's a Rotunda in the middle with North, South, East, and West wings. See the Governor's office with the state-seal rug. Even some door knobs are embossed with the state seal - nice touch. Also, his desk is made from teak decking from the USS Indiana. Sit in on the General Assembly State Supreme Court when in session (older, quiet kids only) beginning in January. Supreme Court matters tend to be dealing with serious, thought-provoking issues. Stories of things found during the last major renovation are engaging. The glass domes above are beautiful to look up at.

INDIANAPOLIS CARRIAGE RIDES
(Downtown), **Indianapolis** 46204

❏ Admission: Average $50.00-$100.00 per ride for up to 4 people (25 to 60 minute ride).
❏ Tours: Reservations accepted. Usually parked in front of major downtown hotels and Circle Centre Mall.
❏ Note: Price covers up to four passengers. Maximum capacity is six medium sized adults, and six adults are very snug. Children six and under ride free with adults. More than four passengers over the age of six, $5 for each additional. Prices subject to change without notice. Price does not include carriage driver gratuity.

Country Carriage Co. www.facebook.com/pages/Country-Carriage-Company/164756893567658

Yellow Rose Carriage (317) 634-3400 www.yrcarriages.com

INDIANAPOLIS SYMPHONY ORCHESTRA
45 Monument Circle (Hibert Circle Theatre)
Indianapolis 46204

❏ Phone: (317) 639-4300
www.indianapolissymphony.org
❏ Admission: $10.00-30.00 adult, $6.00-17.00 child (4-12).

Yuletide Celebration concerts, Family series, and Symphony on the Prairie Summer outdoor concerts.

WHITE RIVER STATE PARK

801 West Washington Street (Downtown)

Indianapolis 46204

- ❏ Phone: (317) 233-2434
  https://whiteriverstatepark.org/
- ❏ Parking Rates
- ❏ $10- 2 hours / $15 – 2-3 hours / $20 – 3-6 hours / $25 – 6-10 hours / $30 – 10-24 hours
- ❏ Note: Pedal boat and bicycle rentals.

Here's a state park for those not in the mood to camp, hike, swim, fish or hunt bugs. You'll find trails, grassy areas, and waterways at White River State Park, just like you'd expect to see in any other state park.

That, however is where the similarities end. White River State Park has cultural, educational and recreational attractions, too. A half mile Riverwalk Promenade made of Indiana limestone offers beautiful waterways, lots of grassy areas and tree-lined boulevards. The Pumphouse Visitors Center, IMAX 3D Theater, Eiteljorg Museum, The Indianapolis Zoo, NCAA Hall of Champions, Indiana Museum, Victory Field and The National Institute for Fitness and Sport are all within the park boundaries and offer some of the best cultural entertainment in the state.

The Canal Walk runs through White River State Park from the White River to West Street and then north to 10th Street. The Canal Walk's 3-mile loop is a popular urban destination for locals and visitors alike. The waterfront is dotted with White River State Park attractions, pedal boat and gondola rentals, bicycle and surrey rentals, and restaurants.

NCAA HALL OF CHAMPIONS
700 West Washington Street (One NCAA Plaza)
Indianapolis 46206

- ❏ Phone: (317) 916-4255
  https://ncaahallofchampions.org/
- ❏ Hours: Tuesday-Saturday 10:00am-5:00pm, Sunday Noon-5:00pm. Closed January and February Tuesdays.
- ❏ Admission: $7.50 adult, $6.50 senior (60+) and $5.00 student (age 6-18).
- ❏ Note: Souvenir gift shop complete with exclusive NCAA merchandise.

The two-level Hall of Champions features four presentation theaters, a 144-monitor video wall, numerous interactive and hands-on displays, a turn-of-the-century gymnasium and a unique view of the sports world via the "Look Up to Champions" video display. From the "who, what and where" basics to our most recent headlines, this is where they celebrate March Madness year-round. The presentations in the Coaches' Locker Room and the Student-Athletes' Classroom provide an insightful glimpse into the world of college athletics. Listen to your team's fight song or find out what it takes to make a champion. Shoot hoops on an old-fashioned half court. Do you have what it takes?

INDIANAPOLIS CHILDREN'S CHOIR
4600 Sunset Avenue (Butler University)
Indianapolis 46208

- ❏ Phone: (317) 940-9640   www.icchoir.org

Having grown to a program of over 1,200 singers in 12 choirs, the Indianapolis Children's Choir continues to be one of the largest and accomplished children's choral programs in the nation. The choir makeup reflects the diversity of central Indiana (singers come from 17 counties). In addition to its own concert series, the choir performs regularly with professional symphony orchestras including the Indianapolis Symphony Orchestra and has also performed with The Chieftains and Celine Dion and at Carnegie Hall.

INDIANAPOLIS CHILDREN'S MUSEUM

**3000 North Meridian Street (30th Street between Meridian and
Illinois Streets - SR 37 North)**

Indianapolis 46208

❏   Phone: (317) 334-3322
     www.childrensmuseum.org
❏   Hours: Tuesday-Sunday 10:00am-5:00pm. Open Mondays too
     (summer). Closed Easter Day, Thanksgiving Day and Christmas
     Day.
❏   Admission: $30-$40.00 adult, $25-$30.00 child (2-17). $6.00 first
     Thursdays from 4-8:00pm.
❏   Educators: wonderful unit studies:
     http://www.childrensmuseum.org/units-of-study

Be sure your kids have a good nap or plan multiple visits,
because this place is five floors of fun! The well-known
museum is as good as they say it is! The largest and most
popular children's museum in the world includes these areas:

❏   THE LARGEST WATER CLOCK IN THE WORLD - Located
     at entrance & a marvel to watch!.
❏   THE POWER OF CHILDREN - The stories of extraordinary
     children in history can inspire children today to fight
     discrimination and intolerance and make a positive difference in
     the world. Hear live interpretations
❏   PLAYSCAPE - Baby area with super soft play/crawl area and
     water, sand, garden, dress up, play house, areas for pre-
     schoolers.
❏   BEYOND SPACESHIP EARTH – Immerse yourself in the life
     of an astronaut. 3 D flight and simulated star. Projection laser
     light shows to modern "hip" music and characters.
❏   TREASURES OF THE EARTH - A 2700 year old real mummy
     with walk-along displays that teach you materials & scents used
     to prepare a body.
❏   SCIENCE WORKS - School-aged children are hands-on with
     the Dock Shop multi-station water learning and construction site
     with stations where kids pretend and play in all phases of
     constructing a new building.

For updates, visit our website: www.KidsLoveTravel.com

❑ DINOSPHERE - one of the largest displays of family dinosaur fossils in the nation. Real dinosaur fossils in a realistic, interactive setting that encourages families to search for clues about why dinos lived and died.

❑ ALL ABOARD! Sitting in the train car taking a short ride on the rails. Speakers and woofers in the seats and video screens of moving scenery in the windows create the illusion of movement.

❑ SPORTS LEGENDS EXPERIENCE - Invigorating, enticing, adrenaline-pumpin with every single step. 12 outside sports experiences and 3 indoor exhibits encompassing physical fitness and awe-inspiring sports history.

NEWFIELDS-INDIANAPOLIS MUSEUM OF ART

1200 West 38th Street (38th and Michigan)

Indianapolis 46208

❑ Phone: (317) 920-2660, https://discovernewfields.org
❑ Hours: Tuesday-Saturday 11:00am-4:00pm, Sunday Noon-4:00pm. Closed Thanksgiving, Christmas, and New Years.
❑ Admission: $20.00 adult, $18.00 senior (55+), $13.00 youth (6-17).
❑ Tours: Daily at 1:00pm. Also, Thursday at 7:00pm.
❑ Note: Snack area/café and Garden Terrace restaurant (Open for lunch only). Pick up an Art Search & Find game at the Welcome Desk. Need some space for the kids to run? Bring a frisbee, pack a picnic, and explore the IMA's 152 acres of gardens and grounds.

The Indianapolis Museum of Art is among the largest general art museums in the U.S., with a collection of 42,000 works that spans the range and scope of art history. Known for Oriental art, American prints and glass sculpture, African and Indiana artists. Popular Art Making Classes or Family Days are a series of Sunday afternoon events featuring self-guided tours, studio art-making activities and related performances for families with children ages 5 to 10.

FORT HARRISON STATE PARK
6000 N Post Rd (Off I-465 & 56th Street)
Indianapolis 46216

❑   Phone: (317) 591-0904
    www.in.gov/dnr/parklake/2982.htm
❑   Fee: $7.00-$9.00

The Fort - (317) 543-9592. Golf Resort and Harrison House Suites & 3 Officer's Homes, plus dining. Landscape and history are blended in a unique setting at the 1700-acre park featuring walking and jogging trails, picnic sites, fishing access to Fall Creek and two national historic districts. The former Citizen's Military Training Camp, Civilian Conservation Corps camp, and World War II prisoner of war camp is preserved at the park headquarters location.

Many plan hikes after visiting the interpretive center exhibits and talking with park naturalists. Others go bird watching for woodpeckers and warblers amongst the wildflowers in the forest. Bridle/biking trails and fishing are here, too.

INDIANA STATE POLICE YOUTH EDUCATION AND HISTORICAL CENTER
8500 East 21st Street (Off 1-70, east of downtown)
Indianapolis 46219

❑   Phone: (317) 899-8293 https://www.in.gov/isp/indiana-state-police-museum/
❑   Hours: Tuesday-Thursday 10am-3pm.
❑   Admission: Donation

To teach respect for the police force or to pretend to be an officer for awhile – here's the place to go. Police vehicles are everywhere - restored classics, miniature police cars from every state or you can sit in a real car (turn on lights, sirens or intercom radio). Also, see displays and firearms; exhibit of Indiana's own John Dillinger; or bicycle safety.

INDIANAPOLIS MOTOR SPEEDWAY

4790 West 16th Street

Indianapolis 46222

- ❑ Phone: (317) 484-6784
  https://www.indianapolismotorspeedway.com/
- ❑ Hours: Daily 9:00am-5:00pm (except Thanksgiving & Christmas Day). Track 10am-4pm on non-event days.
- ❑ Admission: $5.00-$10.00 museum (ages 5 and under free). Entrance into the grounds is free of charge on non-event days. However, during events the Indianapolis Motor Speedway charges an admission fee or requires a ticket to get onto the grounds. This general admission fee or ticket price does not include admission to the Museum.
- ❑ Track Tours: By mini-bus, weather permitting. Tours are $15 adult, $14 senior (62+) and $$8 youth (6-15).
- ❑ Note: Gift shop. Home of the Indy 500 and the Brickyard 400.

Drive right onto the inside track as you are awed by the size of the speedway. Built initially as a proving ground for autos, it developed into the largest one day sporting event in the world and the greatest spectacle in racing – the Indy 500. The Hall of Fame Museum contains over 75 vehicles and numerous artifacts and trivia videos. Antique motorized vehicles, race winning cars, pace cars and even a rocket – boosted car can be seen. Stop in the theatre to view a film of race highlights.

Maybe the best part of your visit will be the racetrack bus tour. Adrenaline is pumping as you make one lap with a narrative around each turn. There is nothing like the view as you approach the first turn – scary normally, but comforting to know the bus is only going 35 mph! The start/finish line has one strip of the original brick track. The black and white checkered victory circle actually raises the winning car and driver high into the air so all spectators can see. You'll also get a view of Gasoline Alley where drivers and mechanics spend pre-race time pampering their cars.

The gift shop has no trouble selling souvenirs to the starry-eyed visitors who can only dream of such speed.

INDIANAPOLIS ZOO/ WHITE RIVER GARDENS

1200 West Washington Street (in White River Park from West Street exits off major interstates)

Indianapolis 46222

❑   Phone: (317) 630-2001 or https://www.indianapoliszoo.com/ and **www.whiterivergardens.com**

❑   Hours: Monday-Thursday 9:00am - 4:00pm. Friday-Sunday 9:00am-5:00pm (Extended Hours, May-August). Closed Monday and Tuesday (December-February). Winter Lights Noon-9 or 10pm. Gardens have more restricted hours, especially Fall and Winter seasons.

❑   Admission: Prices at the gate: $32.75 Adult, $30.75 senior, $28.75 child (age 2-12). Save up to 50%, on select days, by buying your tickets online.

❑   Note: Stroller rental. Parking $10. Gift shop. Also, check out the train rides, antique carousel, feed lorikeet or giraffe, horse-drawn trolley or pony, camel and elephant rides, Kombo safari family coaster, Junior Dolphin trainer (all extra ticketed attractions). Dolphin In-Water Adventures (don wet suits, touch them and feed them, learn how to train them to do tricks-program ~$200 or observers $40). The playground is the perfect place for kids to burn off some steam and, on hot days, cool off. A section of the playground is a splash park. Educators: Animal diversity curriculum or kits:

www.indyzoo.com/SitePages/Education/teacherResources.aspx

The 64 acre cage-less zoo is home to simulated habitats featuring deserts, plains, forests and the ocean. Get inspired in the Gardens by the most unique and beautiful botanical attraction in the Midwest. Highlights are the Water Garden, Sun & Shade Gardens, and, for kids especially, the Motion Garden and the Mist Garden.

Here's some things to look for in the zoo:

❏ OCEANS BIOME - consists of the Dolphin Pavilion, the Waters housing the Zoo's fish, marine birds, amphibians and the Amazon exhibit, and the sharks, seal, sea lion and polar bear marine mammal exhibits. The only dolphin shows in Indiana (performance or underwater level).

❏ DESERTS BIOME - The 80-foot diameter transparent dome allows the animals to bask in natural sunlight year-round while heating and air conditioning vents hidden in the rocks keep the temperature in the 80's. Free roaming desert plants and animals co-exist as they would in nature. Giant cacti, lizards, and iguanas roam the dome.

❏ ORANGUTAN CENTER - Designed to stimulate the apes' physical, social and intellectual abilities, the Center is home to one of the largest groups of orangutans in any American zoo. Your jaw will drop the first time you come face-to-face with an orangutan or watch as they swing up to 80 feet above your head! Lots of unique views but the SkyLine airtram is the best!

❏ FORESTS BIOME - include Amur (Siberian) tigers, golden lion tamarins, and red pandas. Bats, bears & bald eagles.

❏ PLAINS BIOME - kudu and zebras grazing in their large yard along with ostriches, vultures and other birds, giraffes pluck leaves from trees, and elephants or see African lions, African elephants and African wild dogs.

If you get there at opening, you can often watch feeding time. A favorite area, the Waters Biome, has polars, penguins and puffins. The best part is the Dolphin Show. Sit in the splash area if you want to have a good look up-close and maybe you'll be picked to help the dolphins do tricks! What we liked best about the outdoor exhibits was the combination of animals in natural spaces, sharing space with other creatures you would find in the wild. It's like a giant scavenger hunt – seek and find!

INDIANAPOLIS INDIANS BASEBALL

501 West Maryland Street (games at Victory Field)

Indianapolis 46225

❑   Phone: (317) 269-3542, www.indyindians.com

The AAA International League Indians play games at Victory Field, April to early September. The Indians are affiliated with the Pittsburgh Pirates and have been Indianapolis' professional baseball team for a while. If you are able to make it to a game, make sure to look for Rowdie. This fuzzy red bear loves to see smiling fans at the ballpark! Rowdie may even give you a high five, sign an autograph or deliver a pizza to your seat! Tickets: $13-$32.00.

LUCAS OIL STADIUM TOURS

500 S Capital Avenue

Indianapolis 46225

❑   Phone: (317) 262-8600 or
www.lucasoilstadium.com/visitors/getting-around-los-tours.aspx

❑   Tours: Cost is $15 for adults and $12 for seniors age 65 and over, children ages 4-12, and Military (Retired or Active ID). Children ages 3 and under are free when accompanied by a paying adult. Tickets are available at the door only; no advance sales available.

The Public tours of the behemoth building located on the southeast side of downtown Indianapolis are generally offered on Fridays at 11:00am, 1:00pm and 3:00pm. The 60-minute to one hour tour includes visits to the playing field, an NFL locker room, Lucas Oil Plaza, Press Box, as well as other areas not open to the general public.

INDIANAPOLIS RACEWAY PARK

10267 E. US Hwy 136 (three miles west of Clermont in Hendricks County)

Indianapolis 46234

❑ Phone: (317) 969-8600   https://raceirp.com/
❑ Season: March - October.

IRP features three unique tracks, drawing the biggest names in racing from the NHRA to NASCAR and USAC for annual events at the complex (US National Drag Racing, midgets, sprints, USAC Silver Crown and Kroger Speedfest).

INDIANAPOLIS COLTS

7001 West 56th Street (home games in the Lucas Stadium)

Indianapolis 46254

❑ Phone: (317) 297-7000, www.colts.com

NFL Football and the Colts Kids Club package are a little football fan's dream. Two hours before every Colts home game thousands of Colts fans gather on Plaza for a huge pre-game party for the family. There are tons of games and prizes to win in the Fun Zone. Kidz Klub Corner has Free snacks, and Slide and Helmet Bouncer Inflatables.

BEEF & BOARDS DINNER THEATRE

9301 North Michigan Road (I-465 & U.S. 421 (Michigan Rd, Exit 27) just behind the Holiday Inn)

Indianapolis 46268

❑ Phone: (317) 872-9664, www.beefandboards.com
❑ Admission: $57.00-$77.00 per person.A $6 discount is available for main stage show tickets for children ages 3-15. The discount increases to $10 for annual main stage Family Show.

Beef & Boards Dinner Theatre continues to serve up fun, food and fabulous live entertainment. Try a matinee at the BEEF & BOARDS. Dinner or lunch buffet is always included.

INDIANAPOLIS JUNIOR CIVIC THEATRE

Booth Tarkington Civic Theatre, 3 Center Green

Indianapolis (Carmel) 46032

❑   Phone: (317) 843-3800. Box Office, (317) 923 - 4597

www.civictheatre.org

Youth productions each season with its main stage productions ranging from acclaimed musicals to comedies and dramas. Productions might include Nemo, as well as The Velveteen Rabbit, Winnie the Pooh and Charlotte's Web. Tickets average $19.00-$24.00.

MUSEUM OF MINIATURE HOUSES

111 East Main Street (I-465 to Keystone, exit North, one block east of Rangeline), [US 431] to Main Street)

Indianapolis (Carmel) 46032

❑   Phone: (317) 575-9466

www.museumofminiatures.org

❑   Hours: Wednesday-Saturday 11:00am-4:00pm, Sunday 1:00-4:00pm. Closed in early January and some holidays.

❑   Admission: $10.00 adult, $8.00 senior (65+)/Military, $5.00 child (3-9).

❑   Notes: Gift Shop

"A world of small things awaits you". See antique and contemporary dollhouses, room boxes, and seasonal displays. Examples: the 1861 dollhouse, a large replica of a person's home; a $1/12^{th}$-scale museum within the museum; a house all ready for the daughter's wedding and reception; and collections of unique mini accessories. Children can play the treasure-hunt game. See if you can find the dog trying to capture the cake.

DONALDSON'S FINER CHOCOLATES

600 S. State Road 39 (I-65 north to State Road 39 exit)

Lebanon 46052

❑ Phone: (765) 482-3334   www.donaldsonschocolates.com
❑ Hours: Monday-Friday 9am-6pm EST. Saturdays 9am-5pm.
❑ Tours: Group size limited to 20-25 people. Call ahead to arrange.

Donaldson's Finer Chocolates is just a stone's throw off the highway and well worth the stop. Their most popular sellers are Pecan Caramel Delights (turtles), Caramels, and Toffee. Or, you can plan ahead and call to set up a tour. Tours cover the history of the company and the making of the chocolate. See the candy makers at work, and taste the "chocolate bark" that's made on marble slabs while you watch. There are dozens of other treats you'll want to try, too.

MORGAN-MONROE STATE FOREST

6220 Forest Road (8 miles east of SR 37)

Martinsville 46151

❑ Phone: (765) 342-4026,
  https://www.in.gov/dnr/forestry/properties/morgan-monroe-state-forest/
❑ Note: Camping, Hiking trails.

Morgan-Monroe State Forest encompasses more than 24,000 acres in Morgan and Monroe counties in south central Indiana. The forest land encompasses many steep ridges and valleys, and is forested with some of the state's finest hardwoods. The original settlers of the area cleared and attempted to farm the ridges, but were frustrated by rocky soil unsuitable for agriculture.

Draper Cabin (if you can get a reservation). The use of this cabin is a unique experience. No other Indiana state forest offers the opportunity to rent an old log cabin and return to a time 110 years ago when the fireplace provided heat and food was prepared over the burning coals. Three forest lakes, Bryant Creek Lake (9 acres), Cherry Lake (4 acres) and Prather Lake (4 acres) are all open to fishing and boating, but not swimming. Gold Panning is permitted.

BROWN COUNTY CARRIAGE RIDES

Franklin and VanBuren Streets (Next to Old Bartley House)

Nashville 47448

❑ Phone: (812) 988-8230
https://www.facebook.com/browncountycarriages/
❑ Tours: occassional Friday, Saturday, and Sunday from April thru
Christmas season (weather permitting). Half Village Tour = $35
up to 4 people; additional $5 per person. Full Village Tour: $55
up to six people.

Horse-drawn carriage rides. Interesting sites are pointed out
throughout downtown. All of the horses used to pull the
carriages are semi-retired, rescued horses.

BROWN COUNTY HISTORY CENTER

46 E Gould Street, Downtown, **Nashville** 47448

❑ Phone: (812) 988-6089 www.browncountyhistorycenter.org
❑ Village: Weekends and Holidays 11:00am-3 :00pm. (May-
October). Museum: Tuesday, Wednesday, Friday and Saturday
11:00am-3:00pm (year-round).
❑ Admission: Donations

An 1897 Doctor's Office, blacksmith, loom room, 1879 log
jail (men were kept downstairs, women upstairs) and 1850's
pioneer cabin are available on a self-guided walking tour.
The first jail was built in 1837 for the cost of $175. With the
intention of escape-proofing, the only entrance was an
outside stairway that led to the upstairs. The sentenced men
were deposited through a door in the upstairs floor by a rope
ladder, which was then pulled up sans prisoner. The doctor
never owned an automobile and made all house calls on
horseback and with a horse and buggy or sleigh. He carried
medicine and his instruments in a saddlebag. During warmer
months, they offer children's hands on history food and
chores.

BROWN COUNTY STATE PARK

State Road 46 East or West, **Nashville** 47448

❑ Phone: (812) 988-6406.
   https://www.in.gov/dnr/state-parks/parks-lakes/brown-county-state-park/

❑ Admission: $7-$9.00 per vehicle.

❑ Note: Cabins & Abe Martin Lodge. (812) 988-4418.
   Accommodations and Restaurant with indoor aquatic center.
   Nearby excursions are at Yellowwood State Forest (rare trees) or
   T.C. Steele State Memorial.

This is Indiana's most popular state park located close to the historic artists colony of Nashville, Indiana. Indiana's largest state park also has camping, horse camping and riding trails, hiking trails, naturalist services, scenic driving, picnicking, fishing and swimming.

CARMEL CORN COTTAGE

82 N Van Buren Street

Nashville 47448

❑ Phone: (812-988-6011 Hours: Daily 10am-5pm.
   https://www.facebook.com/CarmelCornCottage/

Made up of Indian corn, pod corn, popcorn, sweet corn and field corn, popped popcorn comes in lots of flavors at this colorful shop. They offer dozens of flavors with traditional and double-dipped or buttery toffee or dill pickle…even caramel covered bacon or Pooch Corn mix made just for dogs. Popcorn making demonstrations are available for groups up to 20 children or 10 adults. Watch how they make their famous popcorn, receive free samples and take home a fresh sample bag of their Carmel Corn popcorn. Cost is $3 per person, allow 25-30 minutes, advance reservations are required.

NASHVILLE EXPRESS TRAIN TOURS

Franklin and Van Buren Streets

Nashville 47448

- ❑ Phone: (812) 988-2355
  www.browncounty.com/listing/nashville-express-tour-trains
- ❑ Hours: Daily 10:00am-5:00pm (April-October)
- ❑ Admission: $7.00 (ages 5+)
- ❑ Tours: 2.5 mile narrated tour of downtown. Pickup at major motels every 30 minutes.

Simulated steam locomotive train offers a 2.5-mile narrated tour of downtown Nashville.

T.C. STEELE STATE HISTORIC SITE

4220 South T.C Steele Road (1.5 miles south of Hwy 46 at Belmont, off SR 4)

Nashville 47448

- ❑ Phone: (812) 988-2785 www.tcsteele.org
- ❑ Hours: Wednesday-Sunday 10:00am-5:00pm. Closed most holidays.
- ❑ Tours: Your admission fee includes: Unlimited day access to the historic gardens, grounds, and trails on 211-acres. Steele's Outdoor Studio area, which includes the Studio Wagon and hands-on activities and games. A guided tour of the painter's House of the Singing Winds and Large Studio.Hourly on the quarter hour.
- ❑ Admission: $10.00 adult, $8.00 senior, $5.00 child (3-17)

The site is Theodore Clement Steele's (1847-1926), a noted Indiana artist's, home and studio. See exhibits of Impressionistic paintings by the Hoosier Group painter. Surrounding nature preserves provide inspiration. Guided tours are offered through "The House of the Singing Winds" and the Large Studio where changing exhibits display paintings done throughout Steele's life. The 211-acre site includes four hiking trails, the Dewar Log Cabin and the 92-acre Selma Steele Nature Preserve.

YELLOWWOOD STATE FOREST

772 South Yellowwood Road (7 miles west of Nashville off State
Highway 46 (Follow signs from 46.)

Nashville 47448

❑ Phone: (812) 988-7945

https://www.in.gov/dnr/forestry/properties/#Yellowwood_State_
Forest

Yellowwood offers 23,400 wooded acres with three
primitive lakes, camping, biking, horse and hiking trails,
nature study, fishing, and boat rental. Panning for gold is
permitted in Morgan-Monroe and Yellowwood State Forests.
A gold panning permit is required. The permit, which can be
obtained free of charge, allows for panning gold on a hobby
basis.

Yellowwood State Forest is named for a tree common in the
mid-south but rare this far north. The yellowwood tree
(Cladrastis kentukea) has bright yellow heartwood that is
hard and dense. The tree flowers abundantly but only every
three to five years in the spring with loose clusters of pea-
like, fragrant white flowers. Less than 200 acres in
Yellowwood support the yellowwood tree on north facing
slopes and deep ravines near Crooked Creek Lake.

HAMILTON COUNTY THEATRE/ BELFRY THEATRE

SR 238

Noblesville 46060

❑ Phone: (317) 773-0398, http://thebelfrytheatre.com
❑ Season: (September-July)
❑ Admission: $15.00-$20.00

Enjoy theatrical productions like "Charlottes Web" and
"Charlie Brown". One of Indiana's oldest and most honored
community theaters, the company produces six family-
oriented comedies, dramas, and musicals annually.

NICKEL PLATE EXPRESS

825 Forest Park Drive, Hobbs Station (1 mile north of SR 32 off SR19, West of downtown Noblesville)

Noblesville (Forest Park) 46060

- ❏ Phone: (317) 674-3840   https://nickelplateexpress.com/
- ❏ Season: May thru holidays. Train rides themed for the season/holiday.
- ❏ Admission: Most family excursions are 60 minutes and run around $25.00 per person. Caboose rides are $12.00 (30 minute rides). The train travels through Atlanta, Arcadia, Cicero and Noblesville. All trips are round trip. Passengers will stay on the train for the duration of the trip and will not disembark during 'stops.'
- ❏ Note: Light concessions are available on the train in all cars. Adult and regular beverages are also available. Outside food is allowed on the train for small children or those will dietary restrictions. ***Choo Choo Café*** - This charming railroad-themed cafe is located right across the street from Nickel Plate Express in Atlanta. Before or after your train rides, visit for breakfast and lunch or decadent baked goods.

All aboard Central Indiana's newest train excursion! The Nickel Plate Express is a historic train for kids and adults that runs between Atlanta, Indiana and Noblesville, Indiana. The El Capitan Hi-level cars feature two levels, similar to the classic London double-decker buses. Discover the magic of rail travel as you wind through picturesque landscapes, creating lasting memories with loved ones.

RAIL BIKES rides - White River Family Cruise, a delightful, short rail bike adventure departing Hobbs Station. This family-friendly journey takes you on a charming "bike" ride over the tranquil White River and into the heart of Downtown Noblesville.

GROVER MUSEUM/ SHELBY COUNTY MUSEUM

52 W. Broadway (I-74 Shelbyville exit and head south on State Road 9), **Shelbyville 46176**

❑   Phone: (317) 392-4634, https://www.grovercenter.org/
❑   Hours: Wednesday-Saturday 10:00am-4:00pm. Closed holidays.
❑   Admission: FREE, donations accepted.

Three changing galleries including a permanent Model Railroad Layout and a walk-thru Street Scene with 28 buildings in 1900-1910 decor with Shelby County artifacts. Each room or store is representative of all the parts of an early 20th century community. Fun way to study local history.

SUGGESTED LODGING AND DINING

MAYBERRY CAFÉ, **Danville** (20 miles west of Indy). 78 West Main Street (US 36 west). (317) 745-4067 or www.mayberrycafe.com

The trip into TV Land starts with Barney's Patrol Car parked out front! As soon as you walk in, you're transformed back to a diner cafe where home-cooked food is served.

Many entrees are named after Andy, Opie, Barney, Emmett or maybe Floyd. Aunt Bea says, "If you finish your plate - you get dessert". Each child receives a token redeemable for one toy from Opie's Toy chest or one Opie Sundae.

Andy Griffith reruns are played on TV's throughout the diner. Don't miss the autographed photos of the stars displayed throughout the site. Goober Hat Night is every Tuesday. Wear a hat and enter a drawing to win a free dinner.

There's a varied kid's menu with a mini etch-a-sketch to play with while you wait for your order. By far, one of our favorite "theme" restaurants. Moderate prices. Tuesday-Sunday 10:00am-9:00pm.

CROWNE PLAZA HOTEL at Historic Union Station, **Indianapolis**. 123 West Louisiana Street – zip 46225, 317-631-2221 or www.crowneplaza.com/ind-downtown An active Amtrak station still runs above. Listen for a muffled rumbling or subtle vibration of a train as it rolls through the building. Look for white fiberglass ghost travelers dressed in early 1900's clothing still lovingly lingering about the premises. If you want to spend the night downtown, try a Pullman Train Car sleep room. Amenities include: indoor pool, whirlpool, restaurant and the Circle Center mall food court just a block away.

BAZBEAUX PIZZA, **Indianapolis**, www.bazbeaux.com Downtown Art & Theatre District or Broad Ripple Village. (317) 636-7662. This is an eclectic area with like food. Try an unusual gourmet pizza or maybe a Muffaletta (olive relish...humm - never had it before, don't like olives - but it was good!) or Popeye sandwich. Just their names sound fun. Lunch and dinner.

BRICKYARD CROSSING SMOKEHOUSE, Indianapolis (Speedway). https://www.rootstockhospitality.com/brickyard-crossing Located on the grounds of the Speedway! The Brickyard Restaurant is where you might "bump" into a famous driver or just hang out with other enthusiastic race fans. The Children's Menu has average prices around $5.00.

First, know you DO NOT have to pay track admission at any time, including race days (the 500 & 400), to dine at the restaurant. Just inform the yellow shirts (there during races) as you enter off 16th Street you're there to dine at the Smokehouse. They'll wave you right in. Their regular hours are 11 a.m. - 7:00 p.m. Tuesday through Saturday. However, they opened Sunday from 11-5 for the Brickyard 400 fans. Free parking is conveniently located in front of the restaurant.

45

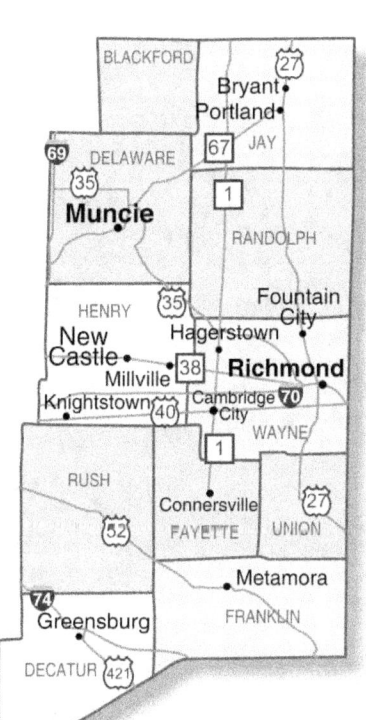

Chapter 2
Central East Area - (CE)

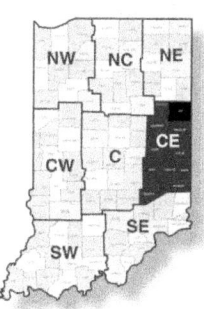

46

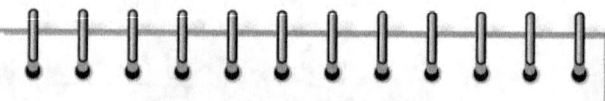

Our Favorites...

* Abbott's Candy Shop - Hagerstown

* Whitewater Canal Historic Site - Metamora

* National Model Aviation Museum - Muncie

* Muncie Children's Museum - Muncie

* Indiana Basketball Hall of Fame - New Castle

Models, Models, of all kinds...

BROOKVILLE LAKE STATE RESERVOIR
3056 Quakertown Ramp Rd.
Liberty, IN 47353 (US 27 to SR 101 South)
Brookville 47012

❑ Phone: (765) 647-2657 www.in.gov/dnr/parklake/2961.htm
❑ Admission: $7.00-$9.00 per vehicle.
❑ Note: Whitewater Memorial State Park nearby has emptied their water basin but still has "land lover" activities such as bridle trails and picnicking.

The Lake is situated in the picturesque Whitewater River Valley. Whitewater rafting is king here, April-October. Traces of prehistoric Native American mounds are still found throughout this valley. The area is known by some worldwide for its significant deposit of Ordovician fossils. These fossils, reminders of a primeval inland sea, can still be seen.

Recreational activities include: Archery Range, Boating / 9 Launch Ramps, Camping, Cultural Arts Programs, Fishing/Ice Fishing, Hiking Trails, Horseshoe pits, Interpretive / Recreational Programs, Marina, Swimming/2 Beaches, and Volleyball.

WHITEWATER VALLEY RAILROAD
455 Market Street (Downtown)
Connersville 47331

❑ Phone: (765) 825-2054
www.whitewatervalleyrr.org
❑ Hours: Saturdays, Sundays, Holidays at Noon (May-October) EST. Special Christmas trains, too.
❑ Admission: $27.00 adult, $16.00 child (2-12)
❑ Tours: Start at Noon. 2 hour stop, returns at 5:00pm. Early train (10:00 am) in October (Thursday & Friday).
❑ Note: Bring a sack lunch to eat while on the train. Sit-down meals in stop at Metamora. Gift Shop with extensive "Thomas The Train" items. Educators: Train bibliography: http://www.whitewatervalleyrr.org/media/Train_Bibliography.pd f . Make special plans for the Easter Bunny Express, Wild West, Civil War and Pumpkin Train tours too.

WHITEWATER VALLEY RAILROAD (continued)

Indiana's Longest Scenic Railroad provides a 32 mile round trip on a historic locomotive #25. The railroad operates other historically significant diesel locomotives and open window coaches on a regular schedule, from Connersville to Metamora. Another WVRR train comprised of a locomotive and one or two coaches operates as the Metamora Shuttle, carrying passengers further South on a two-mile excursion along the restored canal, past the Canal Boat dock, a working aqueduct, and a restored lock. There are vintage Stillwell open window coaches and a restored woodside caboose that ride along the Whitewater River past dams, gristmills and the canal tow path. Great way to spend the day with family and stop over in the fun town of Metamora!

LEVI COFFIN HOUSE STATE HISTORIC HOUSE

201 US 27 North (6 miles North of I-70 - Exit 151)

Fountain City 47341

❑ Phone: (765) 847-1691
https://www.indianamuseum.org/historic-sites/levi-catharine-coffin-house/
❑ Hours: Wednesday-Sunday 10:00am-5:00pm. Closed most major holidays.
❑ Admission: $11.00 adult, $9.00 senior (60+), $6.00 child (3-17)
❑ Tours: Timed, indoor tours and guided help are available Wednesday through Sunday at 10:30 a.m. and 1:30 p.m.
❑ Educators: Lesson Plan for K-12:
http://www.waynet.org/levicoffin/quiz/default.htm
❑ Scavenger Hunt: Fountain City received a designation on the National Register as a historic district. This community, which started in the early 1800s, has a variety of buildings and homes that show a range of architectural styles. From April through October, enjoy a fun and engaging scavenger hunt as you try and find and identify great historic features. Return your answers to the Coffin Interpretive Center for a keepsake! Cost is $2/family.

The Interpretive Center is a self-guided tour that includes an orientation video and exhibitions regarding the history of slavery and abolitionism in the United States, along with local stories related to the Underground Railroad. Owned by the Coffins, this was an eight room refuge and rest home for slaves (up to 2000 total) on their escape North. The stop was part of the Underground Railroad so named because it was a secret stop between destinations. Some would stay a few days and others weeks until they felt well enough to travel on. You'll get to see the second floor hiding place.

The owners, Levi and Catharine are characterized as Simeon and Rachael Halliday in the story "Uncle Tom's Cabin". This stop was so successful that all of the slaves who stopped here eventually reached freedom.

ABBOTT'S CANDY SHOP

48 East Walnut (I-70 to north SR 1 to SR 38 [Left] to Perry [Left] to Walnut [Right])

Hagerstown 47346

- ❑ Phone: (765) 489-4442, www.abbottscandy.com
- ❑ Hours: Candy Shop: Monday-Friday 9:00am-5:00pm. Also open Saturdays 9:00am-5:00pm during Winter Holiday Season. Observation area within shop is open when store is open.
- ❑ Admission: FREE
- ❑ Tours: Wednesday-Friday. By appointment. 3rd grade+. Best before 11:00am, not Lunch time. Fee.
- ❑ Note: First visit entitles you to one free sample of caramel wrapped right off the line.

Founded in the 1890's and still owned by the Abbott family members, they are nationally famous for their homemade caramels and chocolates made from 100-year-old recipes. See the caramels made from scratch. First, butter is boiled in copper kettles and then milk and sugar are added. It was fun to hear the cook yell "CARAMEL!" just at the time it's finished cooking. The other ladies hurry over to help pour out the hot mixture on cold marble slabs. After it cools, the caramels are cut using a hand crank and each morsel is wrapped individually in white wax paper.

ABBOTT'S CANDY SHOP (continued)

After leaving the kitchen, the tour moves into the "chocolate room" where the various centers are coated with chocolate. Cream centers are formed by hand or by using dies and a hand press. Caramels that are to be covered in chocolate are specially cut to size and the various nut and caramel clusters are made in the kitchen using a large depositor to drop hot caramel onto beds of nutmeats.

You'll love their line of funny-named candies called Gismo, Gisnut, Gishew and Gismond. Can you guess which nut belongs in each candy?

WILBUR WRIGHT BIRTHPLACE AND MUSEUM

Wilbur Wright Road, 1525 N CR 750E (just South of US 36 & North of SR 38; I-70 exit 131, follow signs)

Hagerstown 47346

- ❏ Phone: (765) 332-2495 https://wwbirthplace.com/
- ❏ Hours: Tuesday-Saturday 10:00am-5:00pm, Sunday 1:00-5:00pm (April-October)
- ❏ Admission: Tours are $6.00 adult, $2.00 child.
- ❏ Note: Gift Shop. Shelter/picnic area. RC air strip

Wilbur and brother, Orville (born later in Dayton) turned the dream of flight into reality. The interpretive center, built around the replica of the Wright Flyer, provides a look at what the Wright brothers went through to realize their dream. Visitors can read the actual diary of the Wright brothers' father.

The home has been reconstructed and restored to its 1860's appearance, and includes some belongs of the Wright family (like baby shoes and toys). This is where Wilbur took his first step as a baby. Learn about intimate facets of their family and faith.

WHITEWATER CANAL STATE
HISTORIC SITE

19083 Clayborn Street (8 miles West of Brookville, US 52)

Metamora 47030

❏   Phone: (765) 647-6512

     https://www.indianamuseum.org/historic-sites/white-water-canal/

❏   Hours: Wednesday-Sunday 10:00am-5:00pm (April -October).

     Closed Govt Holidays and Easter.

❏   Admission: $3.00-$5.00 (age 3+).

❏   30 Minute Canal walking tour: $7.00 adult, $5.00 child (3-17).

     Offered once or twice a month.

❏   Note: Gristmill on site grinds grain for purchase. Mill
     demonstrations take place at 11 a.m., 1:30 p.m. and 3 p.m. and
     are included in the price of admission.

Originally a town built around the canal between 1836-1847.
Visitors can step back in time while taking a leisurely walk
along the canal path. Along the route they pass the Duck
Creek Aqueduct, a covered bridge that carries the canal 16
feet over Duck Creek. It is believed to be the only structure
of its kind in the nation.

After the canal transportation era ended, the canal was used
as a source of water power for many grist mills. The
Metamora Grist Mill is an example. It is still in operation,
producing meal and flour, much as it did nearly 50 years
ago. Visit hundreds of cute little shops (they made the stores
very small, scaled down, mini-village look).

This is a full day excursion - if you don't mind crowds, we
especially love all the extra activity and entertainment during
festival weekends. Bring a picnic for a lunch along the canal
or dine in one of the local eateries.

NATIONAL MODEL AVIATION MUSEUM/ACADEMY OF MODEL AERONAUTICS CENTER

5151 East Memorial Drive (I-70 west exit 149B, Route 35 north.
Travel 33 miles to SR 67 East by-pass to Memorial exit)

Memorial Exit), **Muncie** 47302

❑   Phone: (765) 287-1256

      www.modelaircraft.org/museum/museum.aspx

❑   Hours: Monday-Friday 10:00am-4:00pm. Plus, summer
      Saturdays. EST.

❑   Admission: $8.00 adult, $4.00 child (7-17). Flying site admission
      is free.

❑   Tours: Visitors gain insider knowledge about some of the most
      interesting artifacts and learn about the role aeromodeling has
      played in scientific innovation and development. Due to the
      length of this tour and the level of technical and historical
      discussion, this tour is **not** recommended for children under 10
      years of age.

❑   Note: Gift Shop with souvenirs plus educational books and kits.
      National Championships in July and August.

Colorful model planes hang above you as you wander through many well-designed displays that comprise the largest collection of memorabilia and flying models in the world. The types of flying miniature craft include free-flight, indoor, control line (lines connect the model and pilot), radio control and scale models. Look close for the plaques identifying world-record holders.

During the summer months, visit the 1,000 acre flying site and see Academy members fly their aircraft in competitions, especially on weekends and during the National Championships in July and August. The fields showcase the only form of aviation open to everyone. We were there for a rocket launch event.... 3 - 2 - 1 ... LIFT OFF! A few moments after lift off, the rocket's parachute floats back to earth. The friendly participants evoke interest in the sport.

MINNETRISTA CULTURE CENTER AND OAKHURST GARDENS

1200 North Minnetrista Parkway (just north of Downtown)

Muncie 47303

- ❏ Phone: (765) 282-4848   www.minnetrista.net
- ❏ Exhibits & The Orchard Shop Hours:
- ❏ Wednesday–Saturday 9 a.m.–5 p.m., Sunday Noon–5 p.m.
  Nature Area & Oakhurst Gardens Hours: Summer Hours:
  April 1–September 21 Monday–Saturday 8 a.m.–8 p.m.
  Sunday Noon–6 p.m.
  Winter Hours: September 22–March 31
  Monday–Saturday 8 a.m.–6 p.m. Sunday Noon–6 p.m.
  Closed Christmas, New Years and Easter.
- ❏ Admission: $8 per person for local residents
  $6 per kid ages 12 and under (3 & under are free)
  Local Residents qualify for our affordable Museums for
  All and Local Family Access membership options. Enjoy
  unlimited visits for everyone in your household.
  Non-Residents: $15 per person for all non-residents
  $12 per kid ages 12 and under (3 & under are free)
- ❏ Note: Gift shop with educational toys and art. Free
  Summer outdoor concerts. Saturday Kids Club.

"Minnetrista" means "a gathering place by the water". Large columns greet you at the entrance. They are the remains of the Ball house destroyed by fire in 1967.

The Oakhurst Experience tells the story of the George and Frances Ball family through the eyes of their daughter, Elisabeth, "Betty". The home is filled with interactive exhibitions that make it an exciting place to play and to learn. The Experience explores the themes of literacy, home food preservation, nature, and time spent together—all things the Ball family was passionate about. Visitors of all ages and interests are invited to come and get lost in a house full of history and wonder.

MINNETRISTA CULTURE CENTER AND OAKHURST GARDENS (continued)

Imaginations come alive in the *Imagination Playground* at Minnetrista! You and your family can, run, jump, play, and create while using giant foam building blocks. What will you create?

Joy of Painting: You can step into the restored television studio and stand where Bob Ross stood, at the iconic easel where he beat the devil out of his brushes. Across the hall, you will be transported to a 1980s living room, the setting where much of the world discovered and enjoyed Bob.

Oakhurst Gardens is the home and gardens of elegant Victorian heiress to Ball Corporation canning jars. The *Discovery Cabin* for the kids is where they can explore nature hands-on. Wander through the *Backyard Garden* to discover colorful flowers, exciting interactives, the goldfish and koi pond, and numerous places to play, enjoy a picnic, or relax.

MUNCIE CHILDREN'S MUSEUM

515 South High Street (off I-69 exit 41 to SR 332, follow signs, adj.
To Convention Center)

Muncie 47305

- ❑   Phone: (765) 286-1660
       http://munciemuseum.com
- ❑   Hours: Wednesday-Saturday 10:00am-5:00pm, Sunday 1:00-
       5:00pm.
- ❑   Admission: $7.00 general (ages 1-100 years)

This hands-on museum is designed to stimulate curiosity and imagination. Longtime favorites like the train exhibit, water table and ant farm have been up upgraded and new exhibits like a weather station and a hands-on construction zone are fun areas of play.

Discovery Park is a STEM exhibit that provides children with the opportunity to understand science in the world around

For updates, visit our website: www.KidsLoveTravel.com

them. Kids will see that exploring animals, identifying animal ambassadors, learning about storm safety and many more experiences are all valuable in discovering science.

Younger ones will gravitate indoors again to the dress-up clothes and take the challenge of climbing through giant landscapes or digging for dino bones. Next, they might build a sand castle, play with waterways or pretend to be a storekeeper in a simulated town.

In the Outdoor Learning Center experience Indiana from several points of view - a forest treehouse, a farm and pond or a limestone quarry.

INDIANA BASKETBALL HALL OF FAME MUSEUM

One Hall of Fame Court (I-70 to SR 3 North Exit, 5 miles)

New Castle 47362

❑   Phone: (765) 529-1891,   www.hoopshall.com
❑   Hours: Monday -Saturday 10:00am-5:00pm, Sunday 1:00-5:00 pm. Closed Holidays.
❑   Admission: $5.00 adult, $3.00 child (5-12)
❑   Tours: 20+ people, reduced rates.
❑   Note: Gift Shop. Favorite (and most crowded) time to visit is early Spring for the start of "March Madness".

The Indiana Basketball Hall of Fame Museum captures the essence of "Hoosier Hysteria" and helps explain to the visitor why the game of basketball has a special place in the hearts and minds of folks from this state. The Hall focuses on Indiana high school players and coaches, men and women. On display are signed balls, jerseys and trophies. Visit the MARSH THEATER, where visitors can experience the emotion of the state tournament. Step inside the locker room to hear one of Coach John Wooden's inspirational pep talks. Test your knowledge of basketball trivia on a computer game or pretend you're playing for the winning shot in the final seconds of a game!

SUMMIT LAKE STATE PARK

5993 North Messick Road (Off US 36)

New Castle 47362

- ❑   Phone: (765) 766-5873.
  www.in.gov/dnr/parklake/2967.htm
- ❑   Admission: $7.00-$9.00 per vehicle.

An expansive view and good fishing will beckon you to this park with more than 2,550 acres including a large lake. Facilities include 125 Class "A" campsites, 3 boat ramps, a beach bathhouse and 2 large open shelters which can be reserved for family picnics and other events. Summit Lake has an excellent bird watching and wildlife observation area, fishing, boating and rentals and hiking trails.

HAYES REGIONAL ARBORETUM

801 Elks Road (I-70 Exit 156A west on U.S. 40 approximately 2 miles), Richmond 47374

- ❑   Phone: (765) 962-3745. www.hayesarboretum.org
- ❑   Hours: Tuesday-Saturday 9:00am-5:00pm.
- ❑   Admission: FREE. $3.00/vehicle for auto tour.

The 355 acre nature preserve with 179 woody plants native to the region, has the 1st solar greenhouse. There are five hiking trails (past wildlife, streams and forest) and snowshoeing in the winter (snowshoes provided).

The Old 1833 Dairy Barn Nature Center has exhibits, a gift shop and a bird sanctuary. The Bird Room offers an excellent place to relax and observe our feathered friends....and a few squirrels.

JOSEPH MOORE MUSEUM OF NATURAL HISTORY

Earlham College Campus 801 National Road West - US 40 West

Richmond 47374

- ❑ Phone: (765) 983-1303   https://jmm.earlham.edu/
- ❑ Hours: Sunday, Monday, Wednesday, Friday & Saturday 1:00 - 5:00pm (all year)
- ❑ Admission: FREE
- ❑ Tours: Staffed by students by appointment. Planetarium shows are given by walk-in request.

Found here are an Egyptian mummy and pre-historic animals. Mammals and birds are displayed in natural habitats typical of Indiana. Hold a LIVE snake! Some highlights include: The Ralph Teetor Planetarium, Indiana Birds of Prey Exhibit, Invertebrate Fossils and Geology Exhibit - displays geological specimens from local limestone, Arthropod Exhibit, Mammal Alcove - displays Indiana mammals in their natural habitat, Marsh Birds Display, Paleontology area - includes skeletons of a mastodon, a giant beaver, a dire wolf, a giant ground sloth, and an allosaurus, and the Discovery Room - with hands-on exhibits that encourage children and adults to touch.

WAYNE COUNTY HISTORICAL MUSEUM

1150 North "A" Street, downtown

Richmond 47374

- ❑ Phone: (765) 962-5756, https://wchmuseum.org/
- ❑ Hours: Tuesday-Friday 9:30am-4:00pm, Saturday Noon-4:00pm.
- ❑ Admission: $8.00 adult,$6.00 senior, $5.00 child (6-17).

Collections of Egyptian mummies (laid flat in a clear chest with push-button lighting for an X-ray effect), Dollhouse, 1929 Davis airplane, Richmond-made cars and a Woolen desk. There is also a General Store indoors and an Outdoor Pioneer Village (site of many pioneer festivals).

WHITEWATER GORGE PARK

64 Waterfall Road at Brookville Lake (2200 US 40 East)

Richmond 47374

❑ Phone: (765) 983-7275

www.waynet.org/nonprofit/gorge.htm

❑ Hours: Daily, Dawn to Dusk

❑ Admission: FREE

Fossil collecting with geologic information available to play pretend archaeologists. The Gorge formed during the Ice Age and has many vertical cliffs surrounding Thistlethwaite Falls. The fossils you will find here are from skeletons of animals that lived years ago on the bottom of a warm shallow sea that covered this area. Some of the fossils you may find are clams, snails, corals, trilobites, and many more. Thistlethwaite Falls is a fun place to wade in the water. Walking tours and geological information are available at the Richmond Parks & Recreation Office.

WINCHESTER SPEEDWAY

2556 W SR 32 (I-70 Exit 151 US 27 north (from Richmond) approx 22 miles to SR 32 west 2 1/2 miles)

Winchester 47394

❑ Phone: (765) 584-9701

www.winchesterspeedway.com

USAC sprints, midget and stock cars (NASCAR) on world's fastest ½ mile banked track.

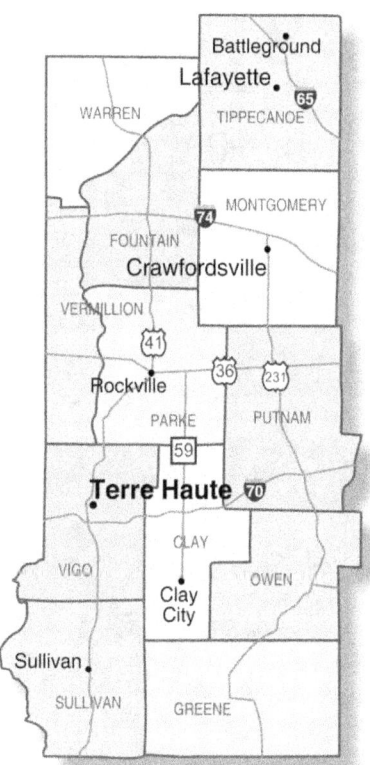

Chapter 3
Central West Area - (CW)

Our Favorites...

* Tippecanoe Battlefield - Battle Ground

* Wolf Park - Battle Ground

* Billie Creek Village - Rockville

* Historic Museum / Wabash Valley - Terre Haute

A Bison & Wolf Challenge at Wolf Park

TIPPECANOE BATTLEFIELD
200 Battle Ground Avenue (SR 43 off I-65, Follow signs)
Battle Ground 47906

- ☐ Phone: (765) 567-2147 https://tippecanoehistory.org/our-places/tippecanoe-battlefield-museum/
- ☐ Hours: Open 10:00 am- 5:00 pm everyday except Wednesdays.
- ☐ Admission: $7.00 adult, $5.00 senior (65+), $4.00 student, $2.00 child (age 5-16)
- ☐ Note: Also, monthly camp-ins, grades 4-6. Picnic/Shelter Grounds. Nature Center open April-October.

A significant spot where (because of the lack of unity between Tecumseh and The Prophet), the American Indian lost his final grip on the Midwest land he had roamed for thousands of years.

Also, the same spot served for a rally in May, 1840 when over 30,000 people followed poor roads and trails to sing the praises of "Old Tipp" - General William Henry Harrison who had 28 years earlier bloodily claimed this battle ground for the Territory. The modern, festive political campaigns of today may have originated from the rally where roast beef, pork, stew and bread were served free. Catchy campaign songs capitalized the great presidency slogan, "Tippecanoe and Tyler, too!" as bands, speeches, floats and tales of the battle added flavor to the event.

The museum has a fiber optic map detailing moves of soldiers and Indians. Two slide shows in theaters explain the progress of events that led to conflicts fought here. The Battlefield has markers where officers died in battles. Your family leaves this site with a deep appreciation of the causes (right or wrong) of hatred and fame of the men who held their ideals so closely.

WOLF PARK

4012 East 800 North (I-65 exit 178, SR 43 north to SR 225 east to downtown, follow signs)

Battle Ground 47920

- ❑ Phone: (765) 567-2265,   www.wolfpark.org
- ❑ Hours: Sunday – Friday: 9:30am – 2:30pm Eastern Time. Saturday: 9:30am – 5pm Eastern Time. Best time is weekends. (May-November)
- ❑ Admission: $5.00 per person. Walkabouts cost an additional $5.00 per person and are first come first serve in our Visitor Center daily.
- ❑ Tours: Recommended. Reservations recommended.
- ❑ Note: Wolf Howl Nights on Saturdays at 7:30pm year-round (also Fridays nights from May-November)... listen to howling, communicating chorus and try to imitate. Weather permitting.

You'll see the herd of bison first as you enter (their faces are so-o-o large!) and then, in another caged area, the foxes (the red fox looks just like Todd from "The Fox and The Hound").

A quarter mile walk takes you and your guide to see the packs of gray wolves in an actual social structure. See them eat (prepared "recycled" animal road kill), quarrel and rest - at a fairly close distance. Learn why the lower class of wolves always get picked on.

You won't leave without an authentic chorus of howls from the pack. Even in broad daylight, those calls are very eerie! The coyote is always the loudest - showy! Be sure to try to come on weekends when the special programs (see Miscellaneous above) are featured. *"OW—oool"*.

EXOTIC FELINE RESCUE CENTER

2221 E Ashboro Road (I70 to exit 23 Brazil/Linton also SR 59 south. 20 minutes from Terre Haute)

Center Point 47840

- ❑ Phone: (812) 835-1130   https://efrc.org/
- ❑ Hours: Daily 10am-5pm
- ❑ Admission: $10 adult, $5 child (12 and under)
- ❑ Tours: Tour times are 10am, 11:30am, 1pm, 2:30pm, and 3:30pm EVERY day (M-Sun). Tours last approx. 1 hour. Buy your admission at the gate before one of our designated tour times listed above. No reservation required for small groups.
- ❑ Notes: Strollers will work on their paths. September Fall Fest and November Pumpkin Party plus December Winter Wonderland with the animals.

The Center is a non-profit organization. They do not buy, sell or breed animals but instead give cats a home for the rest of their lives. On a guided tour you will see lions, tigers, leopards (black and spotted), pumas, bobcats and servals.

On the tour you can get within 3 feet of the enclosures! If the keepers are feeding you can see that process and depending upon the weather/time of day the groups are often playing. Even the cats that live alone will play with their boomer balls and come near the fence for attention. If you love big cats this is the place to visit.

CLAY CITY POTTERY

510 East 14th Street (Corner of SR 156 South and 14th Street)

Clay City 47841

- ❑ Phone: (800) 776-2596, www.claycitypottery.com
- ❑ Hours: Occassional hours but often warm seasons: Monday-Friday 10:00am-5:00pm, Saturday 10:00am-4:00pm. Closed Wednesdays & Sundays. Closed daily for lunch 1-2:00pm. EST
- ❑ Admission: $3.00 per person.
- ❑ Tours: Pre-arranged 30-45 minutes long.
- ❑ Note: Pottery Festival 2nd weekend in June.

Table-safe stoneware produced by a pottery factory. Owned by the 4th generation of the Griffith family. They are the only working commercial stoneware potters in Indiana. The hand-jiggered process of molding (pressing out water) is a very interesting manufacturing step; however, the kids seem to like the raw clay best. The large conveyor drying kilns keep things warm - we recommend tours in temperate weather.

THE FARM CONNECTION

1363 East County Road 550 South (I70 west to SR 59 south to SR 46 & 59, past that to CR 550 south)

Clay City 47841

- ❑ Phone: (812) 939-2813 https://thefarmconnection.grazecart.com/
- ❑ Farm Store Hours: April 1-December 23 Monday, Thursday & Friday noon-5pm and Saturday 9am-3 pm
- ❑ Tours: Guided tours by appt., preferably Tuesdays or Thursdays. Suggested donation of $3/person.

A "Mom & Pop" dairy and cheese processing facility located on a dairy farm. Tours show the area where the cows are milked, viewing the cows out in the pasture, and window-watching as they make cheese.

Even when they are not making cheese, they can explain the process to folks at the store as they look thru the window into the small factory. Sample and purchase Farmers, Swiss and Monterey Jack varieties.

CAGLES MILL LAKE STATE RESERVOIR

1317 West Lieber Road (Lieber State Recreation Area)

Cloverdale 46120

❑ Phone: (765) 795-4576.

www.in.gov/dnr/parklake/2960.htm

❑ Admission: $7.00-$9.00 per vehicle.

In 1952, Cagles Mill Lake was built as Indiana's first flood control reservoir, protecting the Eel and White river watersheds. Mill Creek feeds the 1,400-acre lake and is home to beautiful Cataract Falls. These falls resulted from two pre-glacial bedrock ridges buried beneath ancient lake sediments of the Illinoisan glacial period.

In the 1800s, Lieber State Recreation Area was populated by the Miami, Shawnee and Potawatomi. In 1809, what was left of the great Miami Indian Confederacy sold the now southern one-third of Indiana to the U.S. government, when the 10 O'Clock Treaty Line, which passes through Lieber SRA, was laid out. To learn more about the history and legends of the area, stop at the Nature Center and speak with the Interpretive Naturalist staff.

The state of the art Aquatic Center is open during the Memorial Day to Labor Day recreation season. The Aquatic Center has a zero entrance pool, water bubblers and a tornado water slide. There are also shelters, a volleyball court and a playground. Other family fun opportunities include hiking trails, boat access to Cagles Mill Lake and a campground. The 115 Class A and 94 Class B campsites make this a lovely place to visit. Plan a picnic in the activities field, where you will find horseshoe pits, basketball courts, and plenty of play areas for the kids.

BEN HUR MUSEUM

200 Wallace Avenue (Wallace Avenue & Pike Avenue)

Crawfordsville 47933

- ❑ Phone: (765) 362-5769, www.ben-hur.com
- ❑ Hours: Tuesday-Friday 10:00am-5:00pm.
- ❑ Admission: $7.00 adult, $5.00 military, $3.00 student (13-18), $1.00 child (7-!2).
- ❑ Tours: By appointment year round. Book online

General Lew Wallace built this as his private library and a quiet place where he could write novels such as the famous "Ben Hur." Wallace proposed to write a tale of Jesus Christ, although he knew a novel with Jesus Christ as the protagonist would be a hard sell with the American public. So he decided to tell the tale of Christ through the eyes of a young Jewish noble he would call Judah Ben-Hur. The story would be complete with plots of friendship, betrayal, revenge, love lost, love regained, redemption, and of course a chariot race. He was also an artist, violinist and inventor. Memorabilia include Wallace's roles as a Civil War general, lawyer, state senator, scholar, and artist. A colorful character, he was.

ERNIE PYLE WORLD WAR II MUSEUM

SR 71 Downtown, 120 Briarwood (1 mile North of US 36)

Dana 47847

- ❑ Phone: (765) 665-3084 https://erniepyle.org/
- ❑ Hours: Fridays and Saturdays 10am-5pm and Sundays 1-4pm. (May-mid-November)
- ❑ Admission: Sugggested donation $3.00-$5.00

Summed up by a plaque saying, "At this spot, the 77th Infantry Division lost a Buddy, Ernie Pyle, 18 April, 1945". An endearing man who wrote an aviation column for the Washington Daily News and then became a roving reporter traveling the country. He wrote of ordinary people who had a simple story to tell. In 1940, Pyle went to report on the war in Europe and America's involvement. During that assignment, he was shot by a Japanese soldier. The Ernie Pyle State Historic Site consists of the house from the farm where Ernie Pyle was born, which was moved from its rural site to its present location, along with a visitor center constructed from two authentic World War II Quonset huts. The center features a video theater, research library, exhibits and a gift shop.

SHAKAMAK STATE PARK

6265 W. SR 48

Jasonville 47438

❑   Phone: (812) 665-2158.

   www.in.gov/dnr/parklake/2969.htm

❑   Admission: $7.00-$9.00 per vehicle.

Three man-made lakes offer 400 acres of water for fishing and boating while a new family aquatic center provides swimming fun. Now they have the largest and best fishing pier in the state. People of all abilities will be able to enjoy this great fishing facility. About two-thirds of the campsites are in a wooded area, offering cool shade in the summer and beautiful fall colors in autumn.

Facilities include: Boating (Electric trolling only), Saddle Barn, Cabins, Camping, Cultural Arts Programs, Fishing / Ice Fishing, Hiking Trails, Nature Center / Interpretive Services, Rental-Paddleboat/ Rowboat, Swimming / Pool / Waterslide, Tennis, and Youth Tent Areas.

IMAGINATION STATION
600 North 4th Street & Cincinnati Streets (Downtown)
Lafayette 47902

- ❑ Phone: (765) 420-7780   https://www.imagination-station.org/
- ❑ Hours: Wednesday-Friday 10am-1pm, Saturday 10am-3pm, Sunday 11am-4pm.
- ❑ Admission: $7.00 general (ages 2-100).

A hands-on space, science, engineering and technology museum for kids. See and touch a 1920's fire engine, a butterfly house, a 1910 Maxwell auto or a flight simulator. Now, pretend you're a pilot or fireman. Other activities involve the Art of Science, a rain garden, gearbox exhibit, or Dr. Dino workshops with hands-on creativity focusing on various themes.

COLUMBIAN PARK ZOO AND TROPICANOE COVE
1915 Scott Street, SR 38 (downtown, corner of Main & Scott Streets, I-65 exit SR 26)
Lafayette 47905

- ❑ Phone: (765) 771-SWIM or (765) 771-2220
  https://lafayette.in.gov/1597/Tropicanoe-Cove
- ❑ Hours: Amusement Park and Cove open daily 11:00am-7:00pm (Memorial Day-Labor Day). Zoo open daily10am-4:30pm (til 7pm each summer) (May-October). Park grounds open from sunrise to sunset.
- ❑ Admission: Zoo - $3.00. Pool and rides, $1.00 per ride average. Cove $7.00-10.00 range (discounts weekday evenings).

It's a zoo, amusement park and aquatic center. The zoo has an aviary, "touch of country" petting zoo and an animal house. In the amusement park, you'll find a merry-go-round, train ride and several adult rides.

To cool off, rent a paddle boat on the pond or swim in the 77,000 square foot pool with a 160 foot curved waterslide or the kiddie water playground. From the spiraling Banana Peel tube slide to the leisurely Cattail Crik, you're sure to find plenty of cool summertime fun at the Cove. The Frog Pond (actually, a big pool) features a family-friendly zero-depth entry.

TURKEY RUN STATE PARK

Rte. 1, Box 164 (US 41 to SR 47)

Marshall 47859

❑   Phone: (765) 597-2635.

www.in.gov/dnr/parklake/2964.htm

❑   Admission: $7.00-$9.00 per vehicle.

Turkey Run Inn (765) 597-2211. Accommodations with indoor pool. Rock-walled canyons and gorges along Sugar Creek, Planetarium, Tennis & other Games.

You'll marvel at the natural geologic wonders of this beautiful park as you hike along its famous trails. Visit the Colonel Richard Lieber Cabin which commemorates the contributions of the father of Indiana's state park system.

CECIL M. HARDEN LAKE STATE RESERVOIR

160 S. Raccoon Pkwy. (Raccoon State Recreation Area)

Rockville 47872

❑   Phone: (765) 344-1412   https://www.in.gov/dnr/state-parks/parks-lakes/cecil-m-harden-lake-raccoon-sra/

❑   Admission: $7.00-$9.00 per vehicle. Swimming entrance extra.

Like to look for wildflowers, berries, nuts and mushrooms? Surrounded by dozens of species of trees, Harden Lake is a naturalist's delight.

Nearby Historic Mansfield Roller Mill is a preserved, working example of industrialization in Indiana at the turn of the 20th century. This 1880s flour mill uses machinery from that time to show visitors how flour and cornmeal were processed from wheat and corn. It is an almost complete and unchanged example of flour mills from this time period.

Other facilities are: Archery, Basketball Courts, Horseshoe Pits, Volleyball Courts, Camping, Fishing/Ice Fishing, Hiking Trails, Rentals - Fishing Boats /Pontoons, and Swimming / Beach.

OWEN-PUTNAM STATE FOREST
RR Box 214
Spencer 46460

❑   Phone: (812) 829-2462, www.in.gov/dnr/forestry/

Hike through some of the best hardwood forests in the country. Enjoy deer, squirrel and turkey hunting. Fish in one of the many ponds. Horseback ride through some of the beautiful hills of south central Indiana, including a view of a 50-foot sandstone bluff. Owen-Putnam State Forest offers 6 miles of mountain bike trails.

MCCORMICK'S CREEK STATE PARK
Route 5, Box 282 (CR 46 near CR 43, along the White River, 14 miles northwest of Bloomington)
Spencer 47460

❑   Phone: (812) 829-2235.
    www.in.gov/dnr/parklake/2978.htm
❑   Admission: $7.00-$9.00 per vehicle.

Explore the spectacular limestone canyon, flowing creek, and scenic waterfalls that highlight Indiana's first state park. Hike trails featuring diverse forest trees, spicebush, and native wildflowers, including a trail through Wolf Cave

Nature Preserve and an accessible trail at the recently renovated nature center. Experience history as you climb the fire tower, use shelter houses or cross the stone arch bridge created by the Civilian Conservation Corps, or examine the historic Statehouse Quarry near White River, which furnished limestone used for the Indianapolis Statehouse. Relax in the lobby of Canyon Inn, open to all park visitors, or watch birds from the dining room porch. Canyon Inn (812) 829-4881 Accommodations, Restaurant and Pool.

VIGO COUNTY HISTORICAL MUSEUM
929 Wabash Avenue
Terre Haute 47807

❏   Phone: (812) 235-9717   https://www.vchsmuseum.org/
❏   Hours: Tuesday-Saturday 10am-5pm.
❏   Admission: $7.00 adult, $6.00 senior (60), $4.00 child (5 18).

The recreated General Store, post office, schoolroom, dressmaker's shop, bedroom, parlor, nursery, and toy shop showcase Vigo County history. Terre Haute is the Birthplace of the Coca-Cola bottle. The museum has a large collection of original Coca-Cola artifacts.

Step back in time to the 1950s era while visiting their authentic Coca-Cola themed soda shop! Serving up Coke floats, vintage candy, chips and even coffee drinks, the shop is a great way to end a tour of the museum. Or just stop by for a fun place to hang or work. Unlike the 1950's, they have free WIFI!

TERRE HAUTE CHILDREN'S MUSEUM
727 Wabash Avenue (downtown)
Terre Haute 47807

- ❑   Phone: (812) 235-5548, http://thchildrensmuseum.com
- ❑   Hours: Wednesday-Friday 10am-4pm, Saturday 10:00am-5:00pm, Sunday Noon-5pm. Fridays til 8pm.
- ❑   Admission: $9.00 per person (age 2+). $7.00 more for Ropes.

This new, bigger and bolder kids museum has a bunch of exhibits. Follow your Food from farm to plate, build a house or crawl into a cave and excavate dino bones. Next, create energy, fly a plane or take a look at the Body Viewer. The best part – the tree house multi-level play space with slides and telescopes.

Whether you're traveling across the Deep Burma Bridge, flying through the air with the greatest of ease on the Zipline or wobbling on the Swinging Steps, the Ropes Course Challenge provides a great sense of accomplishment for even the most skilled visitor.

Whether it's a "big kid" testing their courage on the ropes course or a preschooler splashing around in Water Works, the THCM is the place to learn, explore and play at any age and any stage.

SHADES STATE PARK
RR 1, Box 72 (about 17 miles southwest of Crawfordsville, off S.R. 47),

Waveland 47989

- ❑   Phone: (765) 435-2810
  www.in.gov/dnr/parklake/2970.htm
- ❑   Hours: Day use (November-March)
- ❑   Admission: $7.00-$9.00 per vehicle.

A 2200 acre park with Sandstone cliffs and adjacent Pine Hills Nature Preserve. Primitive camping and peaceful hiking trails and canoeing along Sugar Creek.

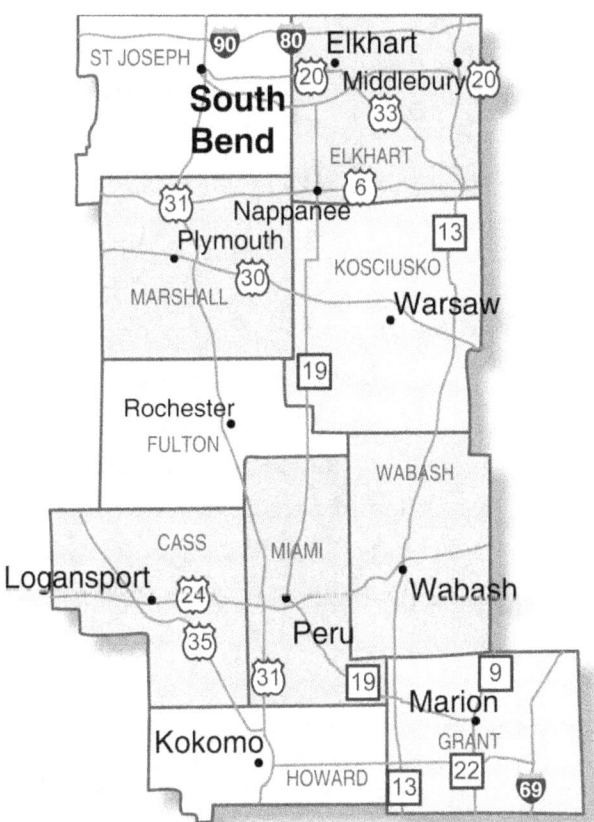

Chapter 4
North Central Area - (NC)

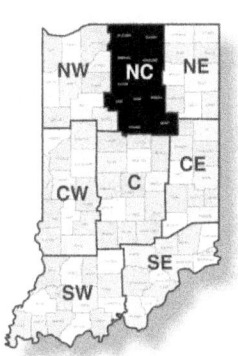

Our Favorites...

* Bonneyville Mill - Bristol
* Kokomo Opalescent Glass - Kokomo
* Manufacturing Plants - Elkhart, Middlebury
* Deutsch Kase Haus - Middlebury
*Amish Acres - Nappanee
* Circus Hall of Fame - Peru
* College Football Hall of Fame - South Bend
* Northern Indiana Center/History - South Bend
* South Bend Chocolate Company - South Bend

Candy Fun! - Lucy, Ethel & Friends

BONNEYVILLE MILL

53373 CR 131 (2 ½ miles East on SR120 to CR 131 South)

Bristol 46507

❑ Phone: (574) 535-6458

www.elkhartcountyparks.org

❑ Hours: Tuesday-Sunday 10:00am-5:00pm (mid April – mid November). Park grounds open year round.

❑ Tours: Guided, weekdays, with reservation.

❑ Note: Purchase freshly ground grains. Picnic area. Milling takes place on the half-hour.

See one of the oldest continually operating rustic gristmills in Indiana (1832). During the 1880's, milling advanced rapidly by using new innovations to speed the production of flour. Many mills were replacing their grist stones with the recently invented roller mill to grind flour. Bonneyville Mill never expanded choosing to remain a "traditional" mill of the civil war era, committed to serving only the local farmers and a few merchants. Watch as the miller grinds corn, wheat, buckwheat and rye using heavy milling stones. The freshly painted red mill and barn /gift shop is a delightful place to spend lunch.

The little Elkhart River offers anglers small-mouth bass, panfish and stocked rainbow trout throughout the season. In winter, Bonneyville Mill County Park offers cross-country skiers miles of challenging terrain and beautiful scenery making it one of the most popular cross-country ski areas in the region. The park's two sledding hills will provide hours of winter fun for the whole family. Beautiful park and walking trails are in the park, also.

ELKHART COUNTY MUSEUM

SR 120, 304 W. Vistula St. (Rush Memorial Center)

Bristol 46507

- ❏ Phone: (574) 848-4322, www.elkhartcountyhistory.org
- ❏ Hours: Tuesday-Saturday 9:00am-5:00pm (February-November). EST.
- ❏ Admission: FREE, Donations accepted.

13 rooms include a Victorian row house, a one-room school, a train depot, a general store, a dentist, a barber, a pharmacy and a tool room. See one of the earliest toy trains made of cast iron or many authentic Native American tools and housewares. Best to visit during an event.

NATIONAL NEW YORK CENTRAL RAILROAD MUSEUM

721 South Main Street (Right by Amtrak Railroad through town)

Elkhart 46514

- ❏ Phone: (574) 294-3001, https://elkhartindiana.org/government/nnycrr-museum/
- ❏ Hours: Tuesday-Saturday 10:00am-5:00pm, Sunday Noon-4:00 pm.
- ❏ Admission: $4.00-$5.00.

Trace the railroad heritage of Elkhart through photos, videos of New York trains in action and two model railroad layouts in the 1880's Freight House Museum. Outside is a New York Central "Mohawk" steam locomotive that's very dark black and only slightly restored (it looks like it could tell lots of stories). There's also an E-8 Diesel and GG-l Electric locomotive.

RV / MH HALL OF FAME

21565 Executive Parkway

Elkhart 46514

- ❑ Phone: (574) 293-2344   https://www.rvmhhalloffame.org/
- ❑ Hours: Monday-Saturday 10:00am-4:00pm. Open summer Sundays 10am-3pm. Extended summer hours. Closed most Wednesdays. EST.
- ❑ Admission: $20 adult, $15 senior (60+), $12 child (6-16).

History of RV and Manufactured Housing Industries showcased in the National Hall of Fame, museum and library. See units from 1913-1960's. The units are displayed in a park-like setting with life-size cutouts of characters in period dress. The museum also presents chronological and technological advancements in the industry from before WW I to the present. The best part – climbing in most of the units to see their varying layouts. Cozy sleeping quarters but convenient.

GAS CITY I-69 SPEEDWAY

5871 East 500 South (I-69 exit 259)

Gas City 46933

- ❑ Phone: (765) 677-7223
  https://www.facebook.com/GasCitySpeedwayOnTheGas
- ❑ Hours: Fridays (and some Saturdays) at 7:30pm (April-October)
- ❑ Admission: $12.00-$25.00 adult, $5.00 youth (7-12), FREE child (6 and under).

Quarter mile dirt track, racing sprints, modified and street stock.

KOKOMO BEACH

802 W. Park Avenue

Kokomo 46901

❑ Phone: (765) 456-7540
https://www.cityofkokomo.org/departments/kokomo_beach.php
❑ Hours: Monday-Saturday 11:00am-7:00pm, Sunday Noon-7:00pm (summers). Weekends only in August.
❑ Admission: $5.00-$6.00 per person.

Kokomo Beach is a newer water park. Cool off in the leisure pool or lazy river; test yourself in the competition and lap pool or at sand volleyball. Zip your way down "high-energy" body slides, or watch the little ones at the kids' slides or children's sand playground. A bathhouse, family changing room and food court make it easy to spend a whole day here.

ELWOOD HAYNES MUSEUM

1915 South Webster Street (off US 31, follow signs)

Kokomo 46902

❑ Phone: (765) 456-7500
www.cityofkokomo.org/departments/elwood_haynes_museum.php
❑ Hours: Tuesday-Saturday 11:00am-4:00pm, Sunday 1:00-4:00pm (summer).Thursday-Sunday 1-4pm (rest of year). Closed Holidays.
❑ Admission: FREE

Haynes' former residence houses many personal possessions and most interesting, his inventions (including 4 vintage Haynes cars). He invented "America's First Car" road tested July 4, 1894 on Pumpkinville Pike. See the first stellite cobalt-based alloy discovered in 1906. While searching for metal to make new tableware, Haynes, in the same process, invented stainless steel. The tarnish-free dinnerware was developed to satisfy Mrs. Haynes' request.

KOKOMO OPALESCENT GLASS COMPANY

1310 South Market Street

Kokomo 46902

❏ Phone: (765) 457-1829 (tours), or www.kog.com
❏ Admission: $6.00 adult, $3.00 child (under 18)
❏ Tours: Monday - Friday at 11:00am (except holidays).
  Absolutely no open shoes of any type due to OSHA regulations.
  The factory has no climate control, so you will need to dress for
  the weather. Temperatures vary greatly throughout the factory
  even in the winter, and can be extremely hot in the summer.
  Parents must stay with children. By reservation only. Max 20 per
  tour.
❏ Note: Broken glass everywhere so follow guide's instructions
  carefully. Gift shop. They offer a unique range of quality hand
  blown glass items including small figures.

Dating back to 1888, it is the only remaining "Gas Boom"
factory where up to 22,000 color combinations of machine
rolled art glass are made for stained glass artisans. Several
ingredients are used to produce this art glass. Some of which
are silica sand, soda ash, feldspar, and borax. All minerals
mined from the earth. The special recipes for each color are
time honored traditions.

The 2600 degree furnaces runs 24 hours a day and 365 days
a year. The process starts when the table man rings his bell
to let the "ladlers" know it is time for a sheeet of glass to be
made. These ladlers use giant ladles to scoop out different
colors of molten glass and spoon it onto a mixing tble where
it is blended with a giant fork. Next the blob is rolled out to
sheet glass form, slowly cooled, and cut to size.

Kokomo Opalescent glass has documented sales to the Louis
C Tiffany Company. This tour is a big *WOW!*

CASS COUNTY CAROUSEL

1208 Riverside Drive

Logansport 46947

❑   Phone: (574) 753-8725 www.casscountycarousel.com
❑   Hours: Daily evenings and weekend afternoons (Summer).
❑   Admission: $1.00/ride.

A restored, working Merry-Go-Round of 43 wooden animals hand-carved by Gustav Dentzel (regarded as the finest carousel artist of his kind) in 1896. The Brass Ring, Band Organ and kiddie train add to the fun.

CASS COUNTY MUSEUM

1004 East Market Street (Jerolaman-Long House)

Logansport 46947

❑   Phone: (574) 753-3866
        http://casscountyin.tripod.com
❑   Hours: Tuesday-Thursday 10:00am-4:00pm.
❑   Admission: FREE

See how the early citizens of Cass County worked and played in the developing community. You can almost picture Judge Biddle sitting at his desk in the Victorian parlor. Would you like to hear the music box? Upstairs the nursery is filled with toys from long ago and the bathroom is decorated to resemble an old time doctor office. Also, artifacts are displayed on the Civil War and American Indians. There is also a log cabin and barn with period furnishings. (Log Cabin Thursday & Friday 1-4pm. $5 adult)

HERITAGE RIDGE CREAMERY

11275 W CR250 North

Middlebury 45640

❑   Phone: (574) 825-9511

  https://www.heritageridgecreamery.com/

❑   Hours: Monday-Saturday 9:00am-4:00pm. Phone ahead to be
sure they are making cheese each day.

❑   Admission: FREE

❑   Tours: View easily through giant windows.

❑   Note: Retail shop. Sample cheeses freshly made.

Cheese Plant: The Middlebury Cheese Company produces barrel and delihorn cheeses with a daily capacity of around 1 million pounds of milk. Cheese is sold to wholesale customers or under the Heritage Ridge Creamery brand at the onsite retail store and online.

Making cheese is an art and this cheese haus takes no short cuts. They start with milk brought from Amish farms. The cows were milked the day before and the milk cooled in 10 gallon cans.

Once at the cheese factory, the milk is pasteurized and placed in giant tubs where enzymes and flavors are added. Giant rotating stirrers (this is the favorite part to watch) separate the milk into whey and cheese curd. Later, the whey is drawn off and the remaining curd is salted and pressed. Our favorite cheese type they make is World Champion Colby - it really tastes better than any commercial brand (creamier, too!).

AMISH (MANASSES HENRY) FURNITURE COMPANY

52886A State Route 13 (I-80/90 take exit 107 onto SR 13 south)

Middlebury 46540

❑   Phone: (574) 825-1185 or (800) 870-2524
     www.ahfurniture.com
❑   Admission: FREE
❑   Tours: Watch production from observation window in back of
     showroom during operating hours. A 10 minute video plays in
     the showroom area highlighting the basic process.

With modern tools, but mostly Amish workmen and women (dressed in their cultural attire), each piece of furniture starts as a pile of pine, cherry or oak boards. They use interlocking pieces (tongue-and-groove) glued together to appear seamless. Now, a craftsman works at his/her bench constructing the piece. Next, it is sanded, stained and hand-rubbed to finish. Try to guess which stage of production each station worker is in?

COACHMEN RV'S

423 North Main Street (SR 13 South)

Middlebury 46540

❑   Phone: (574) 825-5821, www.coachmenrv.com
❑   Admission: FREE
❑   Tours: Monday-Friday at 2:45pm. One hour long. Meet at
     Visitors Center. Not available holiday weekends. Call ahead.

The tour begins in the chassis storage area (the length of a football field). Next see that chassis built into familiar Coachmen Dalmatian-logoed RV's. Cranes lift, saws buzz, and workers tediously wire and install equipment. Learn about their "rain booth" that exposes the finished vehicle to storm conditions (reveals leaks). Seeing the "not so pretty guts" of the vehicle is redeemed when you walk around and explore finished RV's available for purchase. Road Trip!

DAS DUTCHMAN ESSENHAUS

240 US 20 (1 mile West of SR 13)

Middlebury 46540

❑ Phone: (574) 825-9471 or (800) 455-9471
   www.essenhaus.com
❑ Hours: Daily early breakfast to mid-evening (except Sunday).
   Closed Thanksgiving, Christmas and New Years.
❑ Carriage Rides: Noon-8pm daily (except Thursdays and
   Sundays). $5.00-$8.00 per person.

Buggy rides along carriage trails and through a covered bridge are available while you wait for your table. Save your appetite for their famous sweet peanut butter and apple butter spreads on fresh-baked bread. Your kids will be tempted to eat much of this, but save room for the family-style meal and dessert! Walk off all that "stuffing" browsing around the huge bakery, gift shop and village. Mini-golf and bike rentals.

JAYCO RECREATIONAL VEHICLES

58075 SR 13 South (SR 13, just south of US 20)

Middlebury 46540

❑ Phone: (574) 825-5861 (ask for Visitor Center)
   www.jayco.com
❑ Admission: FREE
❑ Tours: Approximately 1 1/2 hours total. Tuesday or Thursday at
   Noon, by appointment. No sandals or open-toe are allowed on the
   factory tour. Closed holidays, 4th of July week and week between
   Christmas and New Years.
❑ Note: The Visitor Center has historical memorabilia and a gift shop.

Deep in Amish Country, this company employs the work of mostly Amish and their dedication to quality is evident as you travel through the factory.

JAYCO RECREATIONAL VEHICLES (continued)

Begin the tour watching a video about the history and production methods of this company, then, on to the floor where you'll see their towable travel trailers made from beginning to end. Starting as a tubular steel frame, wood flooring, sidewalls, carpeting, cabinets and appliances are then added. Lots of wood and metal are used and finally the roof is bolted on.

THE BARNS AT NAPPANEE -AMISH ACRES

1600 West Market Street (US 6 off SR 19 or I-69 exit US 6 west, follow signs)

Nappanee 46550

- ❏ Phone: (574) 773-4188   www.amishacres.com
- ❏ Hours: Thursday-Saturday 11:00am-7:00 or 8:00pm (late March-December).
- ❏ Admission: $45-50 for theatre show, add $38 for Dinner Adults $14.95 for theatre show child (age 4-11), add $15 for dinner. Students half of adult price, add $15 for dinner.
- ❏ Note: Village shops open until 7:00 pm. The Round Barn Theater off-Broadway productions (shows 10 months per year). Evening shows at 8:00pm, matinees at 2:00pm. See website for schedule.

After you watch a documentary film, tour a 122 year old Amish homestead where the family still clings to simple dress and gentle farming. See chores and crafts of a typical Amish family including gardens, orchards and livestock. The village was restored to historical accuracy by Amish craftsmen. It features a long, narrow farmhouse, a grossdaadi house for the extended family, and attendant outbuildings, all original on site. In addition, eleven restored structures have been brought to Amish Acres from across the county, including a sawmill, an ice house, a mint still, and an authentic Amish blacksmith shop.

Farm and House Tour – guided tour through Amish house and farm built in 1874 where kids learn with hands-on experience, such as ringing dinner bell, pumping water from well at the windmill, playing on the old-fashioned swing in the bank barn, feeding the goat a sprig of fresh mint, whitewashing trees, or beating a rug. (April-November, $12.95 adult, $7.95 child (4-12).

The newly relocated and restored German School provides another dimension to the interpretation of Amish society by interpreting Amish school. Experience a spelling bee or Red Rover games. Take a buggy ride and countryside tour. Rides $9.95 adult, $4.95 child (4-12).

You'll have built up your appetite for the Thresher's Dinner at the Restaurant Barn. It's a thirteen item dinner full of family style food (including flavored pickles, apple butter and bean soup). If you're trying new foods, order shoo-fly pie for dessert (only if you *LOVE* the taste of molasses).

POTATO CREEK STATE PARK

25601 SR 4

North Liberty 46554

❑ Phone: (574) 656-8186 www.in.gov/dnr/parklake/2972.htm
❑ Admission: $7.00-9.00 per vehicle.

3840 acres with beach, boat/bike rental, paved trails, family campground, horseman's campground, general store and nature center and exhibits. A variety of natural habitats await the visitor to this park including the 327 acre Worster Lake, old fields, mature woodlands, restored prairies and diverse wetlands offering opportunities for plant and wildlife observations. Cabins and camping (with reservations), too.

CIRCUS HALL OF FAME

3076 E Circus Lane (3 miles East of Peru @ Wallace Circus Winter Center, US 31Bus east, right on Main, right on Rt. 19, left on SR 124)

Peru 46970

- ❑   Phone: (765) 472-7553   https://circushalloffame.com/
- ❑   Hours: Wednesday, Thursday, Friday, Saturday 10:00am-4:00pm (May-September).
- ❑   Admission: $2.50-$5.00.
- ❑   Note: Gift Shop.

If you want to see the best of circus life today and days gone-by, you need to go to the source of the most activity in the last 200 years.

As you pull up, you'll see the bright Big Top and the Circus Museum. It's located in an old circus barn that served as winter quarters for up to 5 famous traveling shows. Going through the Hall of Fame, you'll recognize greats like Emmett Kelly (classic 1900's clown) and Dan Rice (his act was the character Uncle Sam clown). Our favorites in the museum were the vintage circus wagons, painted colorfully inside and out with closets full of even more brightly colorful costumes.

GRISSOM AIR MUSEUM

US 31 (1000 W Hoosier Blvd, near Grissom Air Reserve Base)

Peru 46970

- ❑   Phone: (765) 688-2654   https://www.grissomairmuseum.com/
- ❑   Hours: Thursday-Sunday 10:00am-4:00pm. Open daily each summer. Closed January through February and major Holidays.
- ❑   Admission: $9.00 per person (age 6+).

The outdoor display includes the B-17 Flying Fortress (as if still on alert on a green English airfield), the sleek, fast B-58 Hustler and the fighter A-10 Warthog - plus 12 more planes. Inside the museum, visitors can sit in the cockpit of a

Phantom jet, view a flight trainer, see displays of uniforms, models, survival gear (very interesting), and plane instruments. If weather permits, take the time to climb the tall tower outside and get a "birds-eye" view of the airplanes on display and planes landing and taking off from the base airport.

MIAMI COUNTY MUSEUM
51 North Broadway (Downtown, US 24 and US 31)
Peru 46970

❑ Phone: (765) 473-9183
   https://www.facebook.com/miamicountymuseum/
❑ Hours: Tuesday-Saturday 9:00am-5:00pm
❑ Admission: $3.00 suggested donation.
❑ Tours: By appointment

Miami County history is unique for many reasons: it was the winter quarters for important circus corporations (1880's to 1930's), the Miami Nation of Indiana are headquartered in town, it was a significant site for the Wabash and Erie Canal and the railroads, it has a long military history with the Grissom Air Force Base (now reserve status), and was the birthplace of Cole Porter. The Cole Porter (composer and song writer) hometown tribute contains displays of his Grammy and his 1955 Fleetwood Cadillac. Within the museum are artifacts from a local Drug store, dentist office, penny scales, and quarter player piano.

MISSISSINEWA LAKE STATE RESERVOIR
4763 S. 625E, **Peru** 46970

❑ Phone: (765) 473-6528. www.in.gov/dnr/parklake/2955.htm
❑ Admission: $7.00-$9.00 per vehicle.

Features include: Basketball Court, Horseshoes, Volleyball, Frisbee Golf Course, Radio Controlled Flying Field, camping, fishing and boating, and a swimming / beach.

MARSHALL COUNTY HISTORICAL MUSEUM

123 N. Michigan Street, **Plymouth** 46563

- ❑ Phone: (574) 936-2306 www.mchistoricalsociety.org
- ❑ Hours: Tuesday- Saturday 10:00am-4:00pm. Closed all county holidays.
- ❑ Admission: Donations accepted.

Marshall County has a museum located in the historic Lauer Building in downtown Plymouth. The museum serves as a showcase for the county. The main floor is a changing gallery with thematic exhibits.

Upstairs, some of the former offices which were occupied by early doctors, lawyers, etc. have been converted to scenarios which depict life in the area between 1870 and 1910. There is a bedroom, kitchen, parlor and a child's bedroom with furnishings of the time periods. You can even visit an old time general store where Mrs. Thayer is purchasing eggs. Other theme rooms include: A woodworking room, complete with a log cabin front; A textile room containing fashions and trim from bygone eras; The agricultural room has the tools of the farmer's trade. Plows, planters and cultivators show how hard it was to "live on the land."; A doctor's office contains all of the essentials of the medical arts; and, another unique room reflects the importance of the church in the lives of the county's residents. A chapel is set up with carved pulpit chairs, an organ and a handmade communion altar.

FULTON COUNTY MUSEUM AND VILLAGE

37 East 375 North (Tippecanoe River and US 31 North)

Rochester 46975

Phone: (574) 223-4436, https://www.fultoncountyhistory.org/
- ❑ Hours: Monday-Saturday 9:00am-5:00pm
- ❑ Admission: FREE
- ❑ Note: Gift Shop. Indian and American apparel and toys.

This county is the "Round Barn Capitol of the World" and a central part of your visit is a restored 1924 round barn museum with farm machinery and tools. The museum also features themed rooms like Homes, Toys, Hospitals, Indians, Transportation, General Stores, Schools and Sports, Military, Recreation, Business, Churches, and the Circus. Each room gives you information on little known facts.

Another extra touch is the Living History Village called "Loyal, Indiana" where you walk from the depot to a jail, log cabin, blacksmith shop, stagecoach inn, print shop and windmill & cider mill. The village is only open on Saturdays and during Festivals, except during the summer when it is open when the museum is open.

UNIVERSITY OF NOTRE DAME

111 Eck Vicitors Center (located on Notre Dame Avenue)

South Bend 46556

❑   Phone: (574) 631-5726, http://tour.nd.edu/locations/eck-visitors-center/

❑   Hours: Monday-Friday 8:00am-5:00pm.

❑   Campus Tours: Monday-Friday at 10:00am and 3:00pm (April & May). Weekdays at 10:00am, 1:00pm and 3:00pm during the summer session.

The official welcome center for the University of Notre Dame is the starting point to begin a walking tour of the mystical campus founded in 1842. A lighted aerial map gives a visual overview of campus, and interactive kiosks allow visitors to take a virtual tour of the campus.Watch the 12-minute video highlighting some history and fame, then look for notable landmarks like the Snite Museum of Art, the "Golden Dome", the Grotto and Log Chapel. Be sure to include the "Fighting Irish" football grounds and a snack at "Reckers" (South Hall) food court. The Snite Museum of Art conducts Museum Mornings and JumpstART tours for kids. The Dome has 1250 thin strips of 23 karat gold.

THE HISTORY MUSEUM (AND CHILDREN'S MUSEUM)

808 West Washington Street (I-80/90 Toll Road, take exit 77 on US 33/Bus 31 into downtown. Turn right onto Washington Street and go left on Chapin Street. Turn right on Thomas)

South Bend 46601

❏ Phone: (574) 235-9664, https://www.historymuseumsb.org/
❏ Hours: Monday-Saturday 10:00am-5:00pm, Sunday Noon-5:00pm. Kidsfirst Hours: Monday-Saturday 10am-4pm.
❏ Admission: $11.00 adult, $9.50 senior (60+), $7.00 child/student (6-17)
❏ Tours: Copshaholm, a Victorian mansion of founders of Oliver Chilled Plow Works and a factory Workers Home are on or near the premises to tour. Additional fee.
❏ Educators: looking for research paper material?
   http://centerforhistory.org/learn-history/indiana-history

HISTORY CENTER - Discover legends of the St. Joseph River valley from explorer LaSalle to industrialist Joseph Oliver. Explore Notre Dame's history, pick up phones, push buttons or play a board game of Agronomy. Other highlights were the All American Girls Baseball League displaying uniforms of the South Bend Blue Sox along with actual photos of team members. The "girls" were coached to be extremely feminine while playing the game (this during World War II when pro baseball was cancelled due to lack of male players). Check out the Voyages Gallery – through life-like dioramas and interactive displays, visitors walk along a replica dredge boat and "the Free Life Theatre" tells of the Underground Railroad sites of Michiana. See examples of major manufacturing companies in the area, too (ex. honey, mint production).

KIDS FIRST CHILDREN'S MUSEUM - The large open room takes children on a trip along St. Joseph's River. From Native American dwellings (good picture opportunities of kids sitting in a canoe dressing in costumes, trading furs, tracking animals or relaxing in a wig-wam. Kids can pretend to be pioneers in the 1830s in the log cabin that's complete with a child-sized dining table, chair and bed, plus hands-on household items. Climbing aboard a Conestoga wagon, they can make-believe they're journeying cross-country to their new homestead. An 1838 map of South Bend, McGuffey Readers and hand-crafted furniture give an authentic feel to the 1830s one-room schoolhouse. Very creative pretend fun!

SOUTH BEND CUBS BASEBALL

501 West South Street (Four Winds Field)

South Bond 46601

❑   Phone: (574) 235-9988   https://www.milb.com/south-bend
❑   Season: May-August.
❑   Admission: $13-$15 with discounts for child/senior.

Class "A" baseball team for the Chicago Cubs. Look for Swoop or Stu, Kids Club specials, the newer FunZone at the stadium or Fireworks. The Splash Pad waterplay area is right behind Lawn Seating.

SOUTH BEND REGIONAL MUSEUM OF ART

120 South Dr Martin Luther King Jr Blvd (Century Center)

South Bend 46601

❑   Phone: (574) 235-9102,   www.southbendart.org
❑   Hours: Wednesday-Sunday Noon-5:00pm. Closed major holidays.
❑   Admission: $5.00 suggested donation.

An Arts Education Center with classes and galleries focusing on American Art with a regional flare. Mostly regional works with a strong sculpture emphasis. Youth instruction is offered on Saturdays.

SOUTH BEND SYMPHONY ORCHESTRA

120 West LaSalle (various locations in the area),

South Bend 46601

❑   Phone: (574) 232-6343   www.southbendsymphony.org

Music lovers can enjoy concerts offering six Masterworks, three POPS!, two family, three chamber and a holiday concert. Synphony-to-go and Listen + Learn are free programs offered before new shows premiere.

STUDEBAKER NATIONAL MUSEUM

201 S Chapin Street (Downtown. Off SR 2 or US 31)

South Bend 46601

❑   Phone: (574) 235-9714 or (888) 391-5600
      www.studebakermuseum.org

❑   Hours: Monday-Saturday 10:00am-5:00pm, Sunday Noon-5:00 pm. Closed Easter, Thanksgiving, Christmastime and New Years.

❑   Admission: $11 adult, $9.50 senior (60+) and $7.00 student (6-17). Combo prices with the History Museum nextdoor.

❑   Note: Gift Shop and Science Center Gift Shop. X90 Hands On Science and Technology Center features pulleys & fasteners using principles applicable to vehicle mechanics.

Two Studebaker brothers started supplying wagons to the US Army for the Civil War and then later WWI. Then four brothers formed a company that grew to be the largest wagon factory in the world. Their motto was, "Always give more than you promise". By the 1920's, they were building electric and gasoline-powered automobiles and continued until closing in 1966. (They were the only company that built settlers' wagons all the way up to high performance autos).

See the family's Conestoga wagon, a platinum 1934 Bendix and the last car ever made in South Bend. There's also an impressive display of carriages belonging to Presidents

Grant, McKinley and Lincoln. The one and only white Packard Predictor is in the entrance enclosed in a temperature-controlled case. Can you guess why it has to be in its own case? The Studebaker Super Service Center is a fun, interactive exhibit designed for children ages 3 to 10! Studebaker Super Service Center is sure to put a smile on any child's face as they pretend to work on an automobile.

EAST RACE WATERWAY

126 S Niles Ave (along Niles Ave. & Jefferson Blvd.)

South Bend 46617

❑ Phone: (574) 299-4765   https://eastracewaterway.com/
❑ Hours: Weekend afternoons (June thru August).
❑ Admission: Raft trips from $6.00-$15.00.
❑ Note: Part of a multiple park system that includes playgrounds, picnic facilities, and much more.

A 2000 ft. artificial whitewater course with national and international races is also open to the public. The first artificial whitewater course in North America is a place where Beginners to Advanced adventurers can ride funyacks for 1 or 2 people or whitewater rafts for 2 to 6 people. Observers can look for the fish ladder with seasonal viewing of Chinook salmon and steelhead trout or walk more than 5 miles of paved and lighted walking/running paths along the St. Joseph River. Must be 54" or taller. Rafts supplied but not kayaks.

POTAWATOMI ZOO

500 South Greenlawn Avenue (at Wall St)

South Bend 46615

- ❏ Phone: (574) 235-9800   https://www.potawatomizoo.org/
- ❏ Hours: Daily 10:00am-5:00pm.
- ❏ Admission: $12.00-$14.00 per person (age 3+).

The new Huntington Steam Engine has the zoo's future train passengers anticipating their first ride! They have added some animals to their collection, too. The zoo is so excited about a pair of Takin, whose name means gazelle-like ox. These unique mammals are native to the Himalayan Mountains and western China. And Giraffes! The bird department has added a female Crested Screamer. The African display is now home to Ankole or Watusi Cattle. Each of their massive horns can grow to be more than 30 inches long. The zoo's female Amur leopard received a male companion, Nikki. The monkeys have moved nearer the lions. Australia will be hopping as five new kangaroos are introduced to the area.

SOUTH BEND CHOCOLATE COMPANY

7102 Lincolnway West, South Bend. This is the South / West corner of the US 31 Bypass and Lincolnway (US Highway 20)

South Bend 46619

- ❏ Phone: (574) 233-2577 or (800) 301-4961
  www.sbchocolate.com
- ❏ Hours: Chocolate Store & Lobby displays/Self-Tour: Monday-Friday 9:00am-4:00pm or Saturday 9:00am-2:00pm. Closed major holidays.
- ❏ Admission: FREE
- ❏ Tours: Tours are at the top of every hour. Mon – Fri 9:00 a.m. – 3:00 p.m. and Sat 9:00 a.m. – 2:00 p.m. Inside Scoop Tour ($5.00 for adults, $2.00 for children) lasts about 30 minutes and includes some "chocolate surprises."

❑ Most tours are scheduled by appointment. Tour group sizes are limited to 10 people.

❑ Notes: SOUTH BEND CHOCOLATE CAFÉ (122 South Michigan Street, downtown) serves freshly grilled sandwiches, salads, and soups plus desserts. They have America's Best Hot Chocolate or Fondue for Four –ohh!

The real fun treat before the tour is to adorn your complimentary white hair net and stand by a scaled-down conveyor just like the one Lucy and Ethel used (their picture with mouthfuls of candy is in the background). You must get a picture of this!

Go behind the scenes – where few have gone before. These personal tours last a half hour or more depending on who you meet and where you go! The tours, beginning on the hour, enlighten your knowledge of chocolate and cacao beans. Walk inside the factory to gaze at machines with the molten brown liquid pouring or dripping out into molds and morsels. Check out the big vats and nibble on samples. Visitors then make their own chocolate spoons, eat some more samples and then watch an animated film narrated by Koko, the talking Cocoa Bean. Finally, in the museum, look for the largest Valentine heart box in the world or the 1300 year old Mayan chocolate pot (and Cortez thought gold was the most precious commodity the Aztecs discovered!). Definitely the tour for Wonka-wannabes! So well done and paced at a kid's attention span.

SOUTH BEND MOTOR SPEEDWAY
25698 State Road 2 **South Bend** 46619

❑ Phone: (574) 287-1704
  www.racesouthbendmotorspeedway.com
❑ Hours: Fridays & Saturdays beginning at 7:00pm (qualifying) and 8:00pm (races) (April-September).

Demolition Derby, auto stock racing, formula Indy, classic stock, and IMCA modified.

KOSCIUSKO COUNTY JAIL MUSEUM

121 North Indiana Street (corner of Main & Indiana)

Warsaw 46580

- ❑ Phone: (574) 269-1078
  https://kosciuskohistory.com/explore/old-county-jail/
- ❑ Tours: Self-Guided tours Wednesday-Friday 10:00 am-4pm. Saturday, 10am-2pm.
- ❑ Admission: Donation

The white stone building served as a public jail from 1871-1982. Nostalgic items are displayed in renovated jail cells and sheriff's living quarters. The sheriff and his family lived in the same building and the sheriff's wife provided the meals to the inmates.

WAGON WHEEL THEATRE

2517 E. Center Street

Warsaw 46580

- ❑ Phone: (574) 267-8041or (866) 823-2618
  www.wagonwheeltheatre.org

Wagon Wheel Theatre is a privately owned theatre-in-the-round that has become one of the most popular summer theatres in the Midwest. From the first summer, in a tent in 1956, to the current 838-seat, air-conditioned building, area theatre-goers have seen In-the-Round stage performances of children's and family productions. During winter months, audiences enjoy popular performing artists.

WARSAW BIBLICAL GARDENS

313 South Buffalo (SR 15 North at Canal Street)

Warsaw 46580

❏ Phone: (574) 267-6419 www.warsawbiblicalgardens.org
❏ Hours: Dawn to dusk (mid-April to mid-October)
❏ Admission: FREE

The largest of five such gardens in the U.S., this offers an oasis of beauty, education, joy, and contemplation for all. It is open to all people, regardless of race, faith, creed or physical capabilities. The ¾ acre garden contains trees, flowers, herbs and plants mentioned in the Bible.

WARSAW CUT GLASS COMPANY

505 S. Detroit Street

Warsaw 46580

❏ Phone: (574) 267-6581   http://warsawcutglass.net/
❏ Hours: Tuesday-Friday 10:00am-6:00pm, Saturday 9:00am-5:00pm
❏ Admission: FREE
❏ Tours: Of showroom and manufacturing facility during business hours. Watch cutting - 10:00am or 2:00pm (best times if group). No tours November and December.

Using turn-of-the-century machinery, artisans hand cut pieces of clear crystal using techniques of the early 1900's. Stone wheels run with leather belts in a 1911 vintage workshop. You will see flowers and birds appear in the glass right before your eyes.

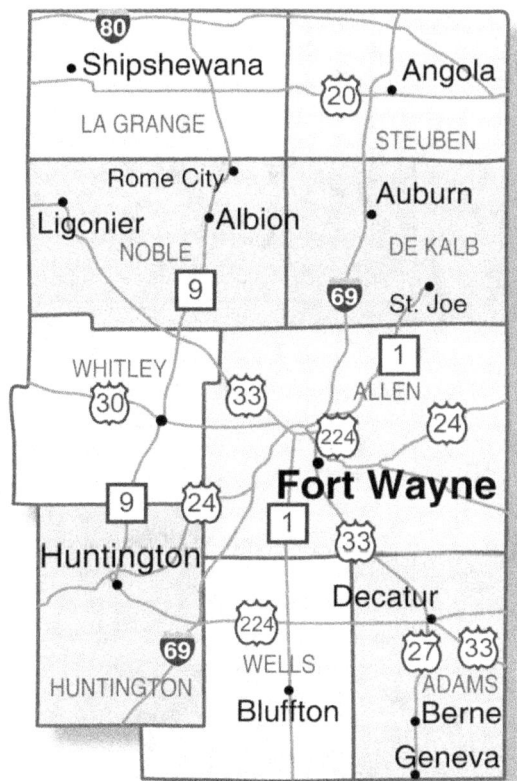

Chapter 5
North East Area - (NE)

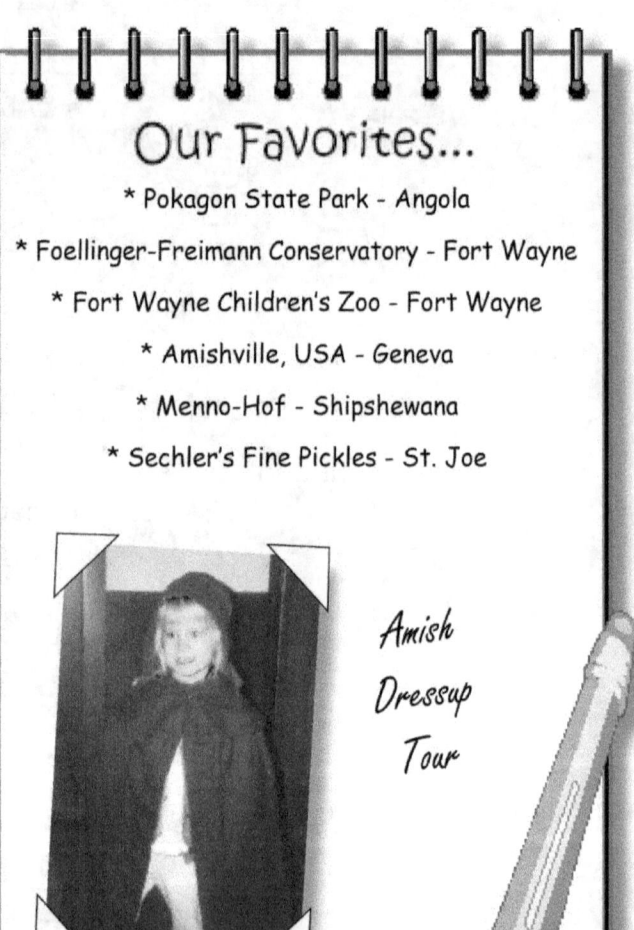

Our Favorites...

* Pokagon State Park - Angola

* Foellinger-Freimann Conservatory - Fort Wayne

* Fort Wayne Children's Zoo - Fort Wayne

* Amishville, USA - Geneva

* Menno-Hof - Shipshewana

* Sechler's Fine Pickles - St. Joe

*Amish
Dressup
Tour*

BLACK PINE ANIMAL PARK

349 West Albion Road (US 33 to SR9 north)

Albion 46701

❑ Phone: (260) 636-7383

www.blackpine.org

❑ Hours: Friday & Saturdays 1:00-4:00pm (May-October).

❑ Admission: $17.50 adult, $15.00 senior (62+), $12.50 child (5-17), $10.00 preschool (1-4).

❑ Tours: offered a few times every day open.

Animals from around the world which are rescued, rehabilitated or have retired from show business are sent here. A unique opportunity to meet (REALLY up-close!) exotic and endangered animals like lions, tigers, chimpanzees, monkeys, bears, and dozens of other mammals, birds, and reptiles from all over the world. Both short and longer, educational tours are available, or, just wander around.

CHAIN O'LAKES STATE PARK

2355 East 75 South (off SR 9)

Albion 46701

❑ Phone: (260) 636-2654 www.in.gov/dnr/parklake/2987.htm

❑ Admission: $7-$9.00 per vehicle.

Eight connecting lakes are the focus here with boating/canoeing, hiking trails or attending a nature program in the park's "Old Schoolhouse" Nature Center. A beach seasonally provides swimming. Cabins, camping and fishing/ice fishing, too.

SALAMONIE LAKE STATE RESERVOIR

9214 West Lost Bridge West (off Rte. 524 or SR 124)

Andrews 46702

❑ Phone: (260) 468-2125 or (260) 468-2127 Nature Center
www.in.gov/dnr/parklake/2952.htm

❑ Admission: $7-$9.00 per vehicle.

Tons of facilities are available here for outdoor adventure: Bridle Trails, Basketball and Volleyball on beach, Cross-country skiing, Snowmobile Trails, Boating & Marina, 246 Modern Campsites, 210 Primitive Campsites, 40 Horsemen's Campsites, Cultural Arts Programs, Fishing, Hiking Trails, Model Airport, Swimming/ Beach, State Forest, and a nicely remodeled Nature Center. The Center has interpretive programs, both indoors and out. The Indiana DNR recently reintroduced river otters into the Salamonie Reservoir area. Wild turkeys have also been reintroduced.

POKAGON STATE PARK & POTAWATOMI INN RESORT

450 Lane 100, Lake James

Angola 46703

❑ Phone: (260) 833-2012 or (260) 833-1077 Inn
www.in.gov/dnr/parklake/2973.htm

❑ Admission: $7-$9.00 per vehicle.

❑ Note: Toboggan Run operating Thanksgiving Day through February with track speeds of 35-40 mph.

Potawatomi chiefs named Pokagon originally owned this land. Enjoy this area as Leopold and Simon Pokagon once did.

Their Cabin Suites are very Hemingway-esk with knotty pine paneled walls & ceilings, antiqued tables and a "writers table" snuck in the corner. Cozy cut glass and leaf relief fixtures add to the castle-cabin feel. Very spacious rooms with numerous windows and skylights plus TVs.

Enlarge your space for more extended family by renting attached cabins with adjoining doors. Great place for family reunions (lots of casual nooks around the lodge to read, play games or have a casual café snack)! Besides the game room, video room, craft room, boat rentals, bike trails, snowmobiling, pony rides, spacious indoor pool and spa, and refrigerated toboggans, there's even more to do around the park grounds! Woodland nature trails leave from the lodge and have themes based on what season it is. Their Nature Center is so interesting and every family there on our visit couldn't resist lingering around and around the many unusual or hands-on exhibits. There's even a tinted window so you can see and hear the wildlife outside without disturbing them.

AUBURN-CORD DUESENBERG MUSEUM

1600 S. Wayne Street (I-69 exit SR 8)

Auburn 46706

❑ Phone: (260) 925-1444,   www.automobilemuseum.org
❑ Hours: Daily 9:00am-5:00pm. Closed Thanksgiving, Christmas & New Years.
❑ Admission: $15.00 adult, $10.00 student. Family rates.

America's showcase of classic cars fill the 1930 art deco showrooms of the former Auburn Automobile Company. Some 100 antique, vintage, classic and special-interest cars, from horseless carriages of the 19th century to muscle cars of the present, fill the two floors of the building. Learn how the innovative cars made their mark on our automobile industry.

NATIONAL TRUCK AND AUTOMOTIVE MUSEUM OF THE U.S. (NATMUS)

1000 Gordon M. Buehrig Place (adjacent to Auburn-Cord Museum, I-69 eixt 126)

Auburn 46706

- ❑ Phone: (260) 925-9100, www.natmus.org
- ❑ Hours: Daily 9:00am-5:00pm (March-November). Closed Thanksgiving, Christmas and New Years. Winter hours may vary.
- ❑ Admission: $12.00 adult, $7.00 students (5-12).

The Museum focuses on post-WWII automobiles, trucks and engines of all years, and automotive toys and models. Over 1,000 automotive exhibits and thousands of toys and models are on display. A special exhibit features 50-year-old vehicles and memorabilia.

PINE LAKE WATER PARK

4640 W. SR 218

Berne 46711

- ❑ Phone: (260) 334-5649 https://pinelakewaterpark.com/
- ❑ Hours: Monday-Saturday 10:00am-8:00pm, Sunday Noon-8:00pm (Memorial Day-Labor Day).
- ❑ Admission: $7.00-$9.00

Experience a full day of water fun with slides, platforms, cable ride, paddle boats, beach, volleyball, tennis, basketball and Concessions. Sand sculpture competition in July.

SWISS HERITAGE VILLAGE

1200 Swiss Way (off 500 South and SR 27. Follow signs)

Berne 46711

- ❑ Phone: (260) 589-8007, www.swissheritage.org
- ❑ Tours: Daily, 10:00am-4:00pm (summers). Saturdays only in May.
- ❑ Admission: $8.00 adult, $5.00 students (rates include tour).

As you enter the town of Berne, you instantly know it seems like another country. Almost all of the buildings in town on SR 27 have a "Swiss look" to their store fronts. The village has fifteen historic buildings moved to one site. The Mill has the world's largest cider press.

Have you ever wondered what it would be like to live in a farmhouse where there's no electricity, central heat or running water? Or what it took to turn cream into cheese? Maybe you'd like to attend an early Mennonite Church service or recite your lessons in a one-room country school? This, and other interesting facts are presented as you take the living history tours.

OUBACHE STATE PARK

4930 East SR 201

Bluffton 46714

❑   Phone: (260) 824-0926.

www.in.gov/dnr/parklake/2975.htm

❑   Admission: $7.00-$9.00 per vehicle.

Ouabache is difficult to spell, but easy to pronounce. Simply say "Wabash"...just like the river that forms the southwest boundary for the park. This is the French spelling of an Indian word, so don't be surprised to hear some folks call it o-ba-chee. Kunkel Lake offers excellent fishing. Other facilities include: Bicycle Trails, Boating, Camping, Cross-country Skiing (no rentals), Cultural Arts Programs, Hiking Trails, Naturalist services (seasonal, summer), Rental-Canoe, Paddleboat, Rowboat, Swimming / Pool / Waterslide, and Tennis / Basketball & Sand Volleyball Courts.

AMERICAN COACH RV'S

1031 US-224, **Decatur** IN 46733

- Phone: https://www.americancoach.com/factory-tours/
- Admission: FREE
- Tours: Approximately two hours total. Monday-Friday 10:00am and 2:00pm at either location. Closed holidays, week between Christmas and New Years, and first two weeks of July.

Children (at least age 2+, no strollers please) and their adults can visit the factory floor to watch the construction of motorized and towable RV's. Highlights of the frame construction (lightweight, yet durable) including studding, welding, joining, riveting and paneling can be seen.

FOELLINGER-FREIMANN BOTANICAL CONSERVATORY

1100 South Calhoun Street (near Jefferson Street, downtown)

Fort Wayne 46802

- Phone: (260) 427-6440.
  www.botanicalconservatory.org
- Hours: Tuesday-Saturday 10:00am-5:00pm, Sunday Noon-4:00pm. Closed Christmas, New Years and Labor Day.
- Admission: 75.00 adult, $5.00 child (3-17).

Even the lobby invites you to a tropical paradise as you browse over your map. Ask the receptionist for the super-duper scavenger hunt and begin in the "Talking Tree" gallery of puzzles, plants, bark, veggies (did you know corn is a fruit?) and a squirting tree.

Next, enter the Showcase Garden where seasonal colors are planted amongst clever lawn art. In the Tropical House come and see an orange tree, towering palms or an Ancient Plantosaurus (plants living w/ dinosaurs). Crawl thru the ground like an earthworm and "slide" into the Desert House. Be sure to look for the cute Teddy Bear Cactus.

Their showcase display has changing seasons (mums in the Fall, Poinsettias at the Holidays, daffodils in the Spring). Did you know a banana tree bears fruit once and then dies? The best botanical garden for kids!

FORT WAYNE CIVIC THEATRE

303 East Main Street (5220 Performing Arts Center)

Fort Wayne 46802

❑ Phone: (260) 422-8641 or (260) 424-5220 box office or (219) 422-6900, www.fwcivic.org

❑ Admission: $29-$41.00 per production.

The Civic Theater performs a wide range of scripts, from Shakespeare to contemporary comedy. Examples are "The Sound of Music" and Christmas-themed plays.

FORT WAYNE MUSEUM OF ART

311 East Main Street

Fort Wayne 46802

❑ Phone: (260) 422-6467, www.fwmoa.org

❑ Hours: Tuesday-Saturday 10:00-6:00pm, Sunday Noon-5:00 pm. Thursday evenings 5:00pm-8:00pm open for Free.

❑ Admission: $10.00 adult, $8.00 senior (65+) and student, $25.00 family.

Contemporary art. A special hands-on education gallery makes learning about art a fun experience for youngsters.

OLD CITY HALL HISTORICAL MUSEUM

302 East Berry Street (Downtown)

Fort Wayne 46802

❑ Phone: (260) 426-2882, https://fwhistorycenter.org/

❑ Hours: Monday-Friday 10:00am-5:00pm, Saturday 9:00am-5:00pm.

❑ Admission: $5.00-$7.00 (age 3+).

Explore the history of Allen County in the 100 year old sandstone city hall (looks like a castle). Favorites include the 1880's Street of Shops and the 1886 dollhouse. Go back further in time to the 1700's clash of Native Americans and early settlers (see Little Turtle's personal belongings and Anthony Wayne's camp bed). Before you leave, pretend to "do time" in the city jail or take a look at 1900's inventions created in Allen County or Indiana.

FORT WAYNE KOMETS

Memorial Coliseum

Fort Wayne 46805

- ❑   Phone: (260) 483-1111, https://komets.com/
- ❑   Season: (October-March)
- ❑   Admission: $10.00-$30.00 for tickets.

The longest continual running sports franchise in Fort Wayne. United Hockey League. Look for Icy the mascot. Edmonton Oilers affiliate.

FORT WAYNE TIN CAPS

Parkview Field (1616 E. Coliseum Blvd.)

Fort Wayne 46805

- ❑   Phone: (260) 483-1111 (tickets) or (260) 482-6400 (office) www.tincaps.com
- ❑   Admission: $7.00-$18.00 per seat.

This professional baseball team is the Class-A affiliate of the San Diego Padres in the Midwest Baseball League. Look for Dinger the Dragon mascot. Promos include Family Days, Dollar Days and Fireworks. Season: April-September.

SCIENCE CENTRAL

1950 North Clinton Street (between State and Fourth Sts.)

Fort Wayne 46805

❑ Phone: (260) 424-2400 www.sciencecentral.org
❑ Hours: Wednesday-Friday 10:00am-4:00pm, Saturday 10:00am-5:00pm, Sunday Noon-5:00 pm. Open Mondays/Tuesdays, too (summer & holidays).
❑ Admission: $12.00 (AGE 3+).

The science/physics playground is housed in the former electric plant. Kids can bend rainbows, create tornadoes and earthquakes, hold a starfish, or walk like an astronaut over a moonscape where you weigh next to nothing. Here's a breakdown of the exhibit areas:

❑ KIDS CENTRAL - A special area just for kids age 2 through 7 and their grown-ups. Discover more than 20 hands-on exhibits including a puppet theater, a captured shadow room, a giant bubble machine that allows you to actually be inside a bubble, a water table and Fort Discovery - a multi-level play structure and giant slide.

❑ OBSERVATION GALLERY - Examine starfish, hermit crabs and other Atlantic Ocean creatures in the Ocean Tidal Pool. Clap into the Echo Tube, launch a wind missile with the Air Cannon, play the piano with your feet, build a self-supporting arch and explore the electrical properties of the human heart.

FORT WAYNE PHILHARMONIC

Various venues downtown including the Embassy

Fort Wayne 46807

❏   Phone: (260) 481-0770   https://fwphil.org/
❏   Admission: At any Philharmonic Masterworks, Chamber, or
     Series performance, children grades K-12 may attend at no
     charge with a paid adult admission.

Philharmonic Children's Concerts are presented twice a year
in the Embassy Centre and are designed for children of all
ages. Concert Kids Club is appropriate for Preschool and
Elementary children ages 3-7 years who can participate in
hands-on art and music activities while their families attend
Philharmonic Stained Glass Concerts.

FORT WAYNE CHILDREN'S ZOO

3411 Sherman Blvd (I-69 to Exit 109A - US 33 South)

Fort Wayne 46808

❏   Phone: (260) 427-6800, https://kidszoo.org/
❏   Hours: Daily 9:00am-6:00pm. (late April to early November)
❏   Admission: $22.00 adult and $20.00 child (2-12). Most rides are
     $4.00. Online discounts.
❏   Note: Lakeside Gazebo. Endangered Species Carousel, Train
     Ride, Safari Ride, Boat Ride (additional fee). Tree Tops Café,
     Splash ponds and spraygrounds.

This zoo really understands kids and their need to have
activity and interaction associated with their learning (i.e.
wonderful rides are offered in most areas to enhance the
"lifestyle" experience of the land the animal comes from).
Enhance learning using globes to orient you to each
continent. Ride by animals in a cute safari jeep or dugout
canoe or train.

On Tree Top Trail, children go in a tiger hut or climb into
the Kids Treehouse. Clean and compact enough for kids to
easily manage.

Fort Wayne Children's Zoo is one of the top children's zoos in the U.S. and highlighted by:

- INDONESIAN RAIN FOREST - Apes, bats, komodo dragon and giant walking sticks.
- AFRICAN JOURNEY - Safari jeep ride on 22 acres of grassland where animals roam free. In African village little explorers can sit behind the wheel of a real Land Rover, beat a drum, and zoom in on zebra with the Savannah Cam. On the trail see lions, bat-eared foxes, wildebeests or feed giraffes and ride the Sky Safari.
- AUSTRALIAN ADVENTURE - Meet a wallaby and her Joey. Great Barrier Reef tropical fish in 20,000 gallon aquarium. Australia After Dark fruit bats. Matilda's Fish and Chips. River Ride dugout canoe tour. Tasmanian devils. Kangaroos. Parakeets. Wiggle through the wombat burrow and get cozy in the kid-sized kangaroo pouch.
- CENTRAL ZOO - See penguins on parade, beautiful multicolored macaws, the capuchin monkeys on monkey island, and giant tortoises. At Sea Lion Beach you'll see the sea lions as you've never seen them before. Indiana Family Farm area, where you can hug a goat, pet a cow, and see the baby chicks. Everyone will enjoy a ride on a 1860's miniature train.

DEBRAND CHOCOLATES
Corporate Hdqtrs, 10105 Auburn Park Dr (I-69 exit 116, Dupont Rd)

Fort Wayne 46825

- Phone: (260) 969-8335 or www.debrand.com
- Hours: Daily morning until dark. Basic retail hours.
- Tours: Tuesday at 10am and Thursdays at 1pm. Also, Saturdays at 10:30am. Depending on attendance levels, tours typically last 45 minutes. Tours are handicapped accessible. Cost is $10 per person, with each person receiving a rebate of $10 off a $20 or more purchase.

Another great chocolate factory tour in the Midwest! Tours begin with a 15-minute video. Groups are then led to begin the tour. You'll start with a tour guide telling you about their three DeBrand chocolate kitchens. There you will learn about the delicate chocolate making process, watching these artisan chocolates being hand-made and sampling some exquisite chocolates. End the tour in their elegant shoppe where you can use your admission certificate to purchase some of these treats…or sit and order delicious desserts and drinks.

FIREFIGHTERS' MUSEUM

226 West Washington Blvd.

Fort Wayne 46802

- ❑   Phone: (260) 426-0051
    www.fortwaynefiremuseum.com
- ❑   Hours: Monday-Friday 10:00am-4:00pm, Saturdays 10:00am-3:00pm. Closed Wednesdays, Sundays & Holidays.
- ❑   Admission: $5.00-$6.00 (age 3+).

The museum showcases artifacts used by some of the city's earliest heroes - the firefighters. It has preserved the history of the Fort Wayne Fire Department and also gives tours (by appointment) to teach fire safety. Say "Hi" to the Dalmatian.

WILD WINDS BUFFALO PRESERVE

6975 N. Ray St. (I-80/90 east towards tri-state border. Exit SR 120/827. Follow signs east)

Fremont 46737

- ❑   Phone: (260) 495-0137
    https://www.facebook.com/wildwindsbuffalopreserve.net/
- ❑   Hours: Wednesday-Sunday 10:00am-4:00pm (April-December). Saturday only January – March.
- ❑   Tours: Tours available to general public and walk-ins are welcome. Guided tours into the bison herd: $10 adults, $7 under 10 yrs old, free under 2 yrs. Several times daily.

Wild Winds Buffalo Preserve offers a taste of the West right here in the Midwest. The site offers over 400 sacred acres of rolling Indiana Prairie Land, natural Water Ways, Lakes, Birds and home to approximately 200 Bison. Take a tour right into the field with the bison by vehicle or take a scenic property tour by horseback. Tour the preserve on horseback, or use the walking trails. A stay at the bed and breakfast includes the comforts of a pine cabin and a "Buffalo Breakfast." Step back in time and relax. There are no computers or fax machines, TV or public phones to disrupt your experience.

AMISHVILLE USA
844 East 900 South (1-69 to Highway 218 to US 27 - Follow signs from Berne)

Geneva 46740

❑   Phone: (260) 589-3536,
      https://www.facebook.com/AmishvilleUSA/
❑   Note: Gift Shop. Amishville Grille (eating place) - Amish &
      Swiss recipes and Country Harvest Buffet (moderate pricing,
      open Fridays & Saturdays for lunch and dinner). Working
      Gristmill on premises (can even buy product). Campsites on
      property available. Saturday evenings planned activities. The
      Barn with live farm animals is available to visit when the
      campground is open. Season is Spring thru mid-Fall.

The tales of an Old Order Amish home life is the highlight of this visit. Ask locals for descriptions of a typical day - for instance, Sally would go fetch eggs while Johnny would milk cows or feed horses. Pins and occasional buttons are used in clothing - never shiny zippers. See how families survive without electricity or plumbing and how close the families are (grandparents live in a house next to the main house). Set back on a country road lined with traditional Amish farms and buggies as people go about their daily chores. Truly authentic "Amish-cana"!

LIMBERLOST STATE HISTORIC SITE

200 East 6th Street (one block east of US 27)

Geneva 46740

- ❑ Phone: (260) 368-7428 https://www.indianamuseum.org/historic-sites/limberlost/
- ❑ Hours: Wednesday-Sunday 9:00am-5:00pm. Tours at 11:00am, 1:00pm & 3:00pm. Closed Thanksgiving, Christmastime, New Years and Easter. Closed mid-December thru March.
- ❑ Admission: $8 adult, $7 senior (60+), $5 child (3-17).

13,000 acres across the vast forest and swampland was a legend for its quicksand and unsavory characters. The swamp received its name from the fate of Limber Jim Corbus, who went hunting in the swamp and never returned. When the locals asked where Jim Corbus was, the familiar cry was "Limber's lost!" To Gene Stratton-Porter, the swamp was her playground, laboratory and inspiration. The swamp was the subject of her acclaimed books and photographs.

ANTIQOLOGY

401 N. Jefferson (I-69 at US 224 or US 24 exit)

Huntington 46750

- ❑ https://www.facebook.com/Antiqology/
- ❑ Hours: Wednesday-Thursday 10am-7pm, Friday-Saturday 10am-9pm, Sunday Noon-7pm.

It combines antiques, soda, and ice cream. Eclectic would be a great word for the store's antiques. And, everyone should get the chance to have a Strawberry Fanta float at least once in their lifetime!

THE QUAYLE VICE PRESIDENTIAL LEARNING CENTER

815 Warren Street (I-69 at US 224 or US 24 exit - Downtown corner of Warren and Tipton Streets)

Huntington 46750

❑   Phone: (260) 356-6356, https://historyeducates.org/
❑   Hours: Tuesday-Friday 10:00am-3:00pm, Saturday 9:00am-1:00pm. Closed major holidays.
❑   Admission: $5.00 adult, $2.00 child (7-17).

America's only Vice-Presidential museum specifically dedicated to J. Danforth Quayle, 44th Vice-President. Trace Quayle's early years growing up in Huntington along with his political career. See his report card from local schools and pictures with Presidents. Exhibits and programs focus on the history and politics behind our nation's Vice-Presidents with spotlights on the five Vice-Presidents from Indiana. Large screen video presentation. Gift Shop.

FORKS OF THE WABASH HISTORIC PARK

3010 West Park Drive (U524 and SR 9)

Huntington 46750

❑   Phone: (260) 356-1903, http://forksofthewabash.org/
❑   Hours: Open Tuesday and Thursday mornings. Weekends special events. Not open to the public for tours, only private and scheduled school tours. $8.00 per person for tours.

Start your visit of the museum and historical park that tells the story of the relationship between early European settlers and the Miami Indians (trading) and the US Government (treaties). The park includes a log schoolhouse, family pioneer house of German farmers and most interestingly, the home of Miami Chief Richardville. The chief was considered a skilled negotiator in treaty talks and the wealthiest Native American in North America at his death. Families can take part in their special events on pioneer life (see events listings for details).

HUNTINGTON LAKE STATE RESERVOIR

517 North Warren Road (off Rte. 5)

Huntington 46750

- ❑ Phone: (260) 468-2165 www.in.gov/dnr/parklake/2956.htm
- ❑ Admission: $7-$9.00 per vehicle

J. Edward Roush Lake. Archery Range, Basketball Courts, Mountain Bike Trail, Horseshoes & Croquet, Model Airport, Volleyball Courts on beach.

MID-AMERICA WINDMILL MUSEUM

732 S Allen Chapel Rd, **Kendallville** 46755

- ❑ Phone: (260) 347-2334 www.midamericawindmillmuseum.org
- ❑ Hours: Tuesday-Friday 10:00am-4:00pm, Saturday 10:00am-5:00pm. Sunday 1:00-4:00 pm (April-November)
- ❑ Admission: $3.00-$5.00

Take a peek at the past of energy generation and self-reliance of the Midwest and Great Plains represented by windmills that once served settlers as they went westward. The development of the west was won thanks to the power generated by windmills that utilized breezes and coaxed water to the surface.

The Kendallville area was home to many windmill manufacturers. The museum demonstrates the windmill's heritage through a video on wind power, more than 50 windmills on the museum's 40-acre grounds, and an 1880s barn.

GENE STRATTON PORTER STATE HISTORIC SITE

1205 Pleasant Point (5 miles west of Kendallville on US 6 and 3 miles north on SR 9), **Kendallville** (**Rome City**) 46784

- ❑ Phone: (260) 854-3790
  https://www.indianamuseum.org/historic-sites/gene-stratton-porter/

❑ Hours: Wednesday-Sunday 10:00am-5:00pm (April-November). Closed Thanksgiving, Christmastime, New Years and Easter.

❑ Admission: $8 adult, $7 senior (60+), $5 child (3-17).

❑ Tours: Guided Cabin Tours at 11:00am, 1:00pm and 3:00pm.

"The Cabin in the Wildflower Woods" lies nestled on the shore of Sylvan Lake, near Rome City, Indiana. It is the second Indiana home of Hoosier author, naturalist, photographer, Gene Stratton Porter. In her lifetime, 1863-1924, Porter authored 12 novels, seven nature books, two books of poetry, children's books and numerous magazine articles. Eight of her novels were produced as motion pictures.

Furnishings in the home are arranged and maintained to reflect, as authentically as possible, the Porter's lifestyle. Located on beautiful Sylvan lake, you can hike through the woods, stroll through the gardens and rest on a bench under a shade tree...or bring a picnic at the facilities. You can take a cruise on the pontoon boat for a nominal fee. There is access to the lake; however, no boat ramp is provided. Hike a nearby mile–long trail and see the manager's home and barn.

BUGGY LANE TOURS
(SR 5, across from flea market)
Shipshewana 46565

❑ Phone: (574) 333-9584   http://www.buggylanetours.com/

❑ Admission: $8.00 per person (ride only). $12.00 - 15 minute tour. $23.00 half hour tour. $18.00-$35.00 for 1.5 to 2 hour hands-on tour.

❑ Tours: May thru December Monday-Saturday 10am-Dusk. Buggy rides between 10:00am-4:30pm.

Buggy rides, back roads country tours (in 15 passenger buggies), step-on guides and Amish farm tours.

BUGGY LANE TOURS (continued)

On tour, maybe stop at the buggy shop to see what's involved in making a buggy. How about a Loom Shop? Ever think about how long it takes to make a terrific rug or table runner? Of course, you haven't seen anything until you see the Country Store or had an authentic Amish Dinner.

While you are touring, you'll hear many stories of the Amish heritage. You are encouraged to ask questions, so that you can understand their way of living better.

MENNO-HOF, MENNONITE-AMISH VISITORS CENTER

510 South Van Buren Street (North of US 20 and SR 5)

Shipshewana 46565

- ❏ Phone: (260) 768-4117, www.mennohof.org
- ❏ Hours: Monday-Saturday 10:00am-5:00pm. (Adjusted seasonally, especially Winter)
- ❏ Admission: $8.50 adult, $5.00 child (6-14), $18 family.
- ❏ Tours: One hour, start every 15 minutes.
- ❏ Note: Most of the tour is "over the heads" of children twelve years and under; however, you can advise your guide of this and they can accommodate by spending significant time in the Interactive Room.

Where can you take one journey starting in a courtyard in 1525, in Europe, around a water pitcher? Then, get locked in a dungeon, escape in a "cramped quarters" ship, survive a tornado and learn about the power of faith! About halfway through, children will have the chance to walk around and play in an Amish built (beams, pegs and kneebraces only) barn stocked with simple wood toys. Our kids had to be pulled away - we may never buy "gadget" toys again! This is a very thorough walking tour of the story of tragedy and triumph of a people searching for peace. Afterwards, you'll truly understand the reasons for their way of life.

SECHLER'S FINE PICKLES

5686 SR 1 (1-69 North to DuPont Exit to SR 1 North - 20 miles)

St. Joe 46785

❑ Phone: (260) 337-5461

www.sechlerspickles.com

❑ Admission: FREE

❑ Tours: Monday-Thursday 9:00-11:00am & 12:30-3:00pm (April-October). Tours every half hour.

❑ Showroom open weekdays until 4:30pm. Saturday 8:30am-Noon. Groups of 6 or more need reservations.

❑ Note: Retail showroom has sample table with one of each variety pickle available to taste. Try flavors like jalapeno slices, orange or candied raisin crispies.

Pucker up for pickles! 39 Flavors! (That's pickles, not ice cream, of course) Ralph Sechler began pickle processing in 1921 in his home (next to the factory). Pickles are just cucumbers, salt, water, vinegar and spices but the secret combination prepares just the right taste.

Around the side of the building, you might see truckloads of "cukes" arrive (farmers are paid the highest price for "gherkins", the smallest) and sorted into slots for seven different sizes. Each size is processed in covered vats full of salt brine for 2½ months to 1½ years depending upon demand. Before pickles are packaged, they are first cooked for 24 hours, then sliced, chopped or ground and left to marinate 1-10 days in special spice solutions. Workers stand by special stainless steel tables and hand-pack each variety in its special brine. Our favorite flavor is sweet apple cinnamon. Be sure to take some of the 39 varieties home!

SUGGESTED LODGING AND DINING

PIZZA JUNCTION - **Huntington**, 201 Court Street
(between courthouse & railroad tracks). (260) 356-4700.
https://www.facebook.com/pizzajunctioncafe/ Open daily
for lunch and dinner. Located by the railroad tracks in a
restored train depot. It's really fun when a train goes past.
Actual restored photos of historic buildings around town
(like Nick's Kitchen) and the original freight depot.

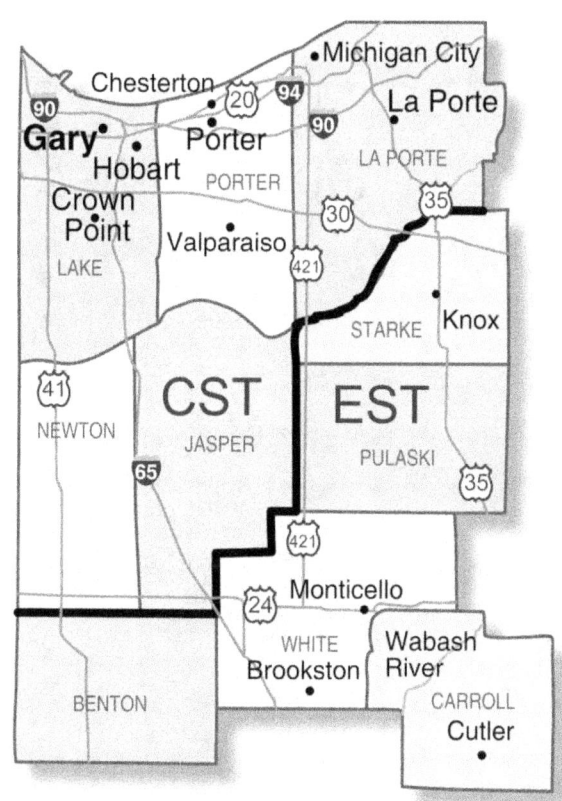

Chapter 6
North West Area - (NW)

Our Favorites...

* Twinrocker Handmade Paper - Brookston

* Indiana Dunes State Park &
  National Lakeshore - Chesterton

* Wabash & Erie Canal Park - Delphi

* Waterparks

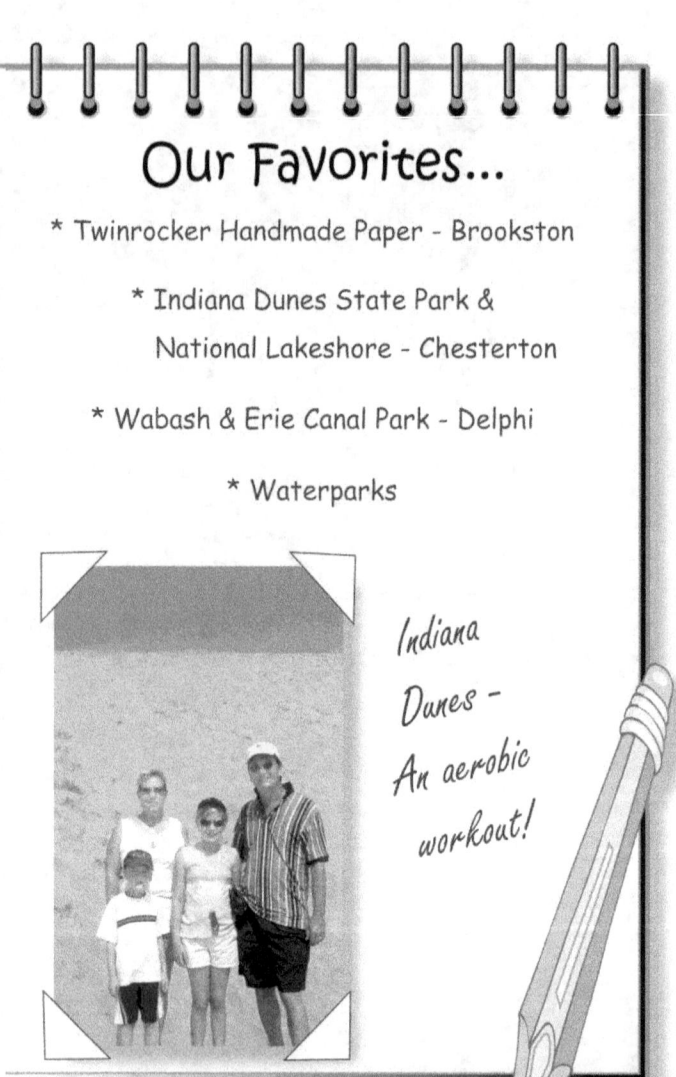

Indiana Dunes - An aerobic workout!

TWINROCKER HANDMADE PAPER
100 East Third Street (downtown, by railroad tracks)

Brookston 47923

❑   Phone: (765) 563-3119 or (800)757-TWIN
www.twinrocker.com

❑   Hours: Monday-Friday 9:00am-3:00pm

❑   Admission: $4.00/person for school age children and older, minimum of $48 for the group.

❑   Tours: By appointment Monday-Thursday 10am-2pm.

❑   Note: All handmade papers are discounted 25% for the tour group. ("Seconds" are discounted 30 to 50%).

The painstaking, lost art of making sheet paper by hand is back. Twinrocker was among the first hand mills to open in the 70's. Watch "cooked" cotton, husk or linen rag fibers turn into custom paper.

Individuals, families, and small and large groups up to 70 are welcome to visit Twinrocker to take a tour of the paper studio. A Twinrocker staff member will speak to your group about the history and practice of this ancient craft while you watch them at work. You'll see them first beat the fiber with water. We learned this releases cellulose causing fiber and water to bond. Next a mold or sieve is dipped into the vat of pulp and shaken. The new sheet formed is "couched" between pieces of wool felt, pressed and then dried. As the paper dries and water evaporates, the fibers bond closer. A special copywritten exaggerated "Feather" deckle edge is the company signature.

Visitors are welcome to see the large selection of papers for watercolor, pastel, calligraphy, printmaking, drawing and stationery.

INDIANA DUNES STATE PARK/ NATIONAL LAKESHORE

1600 N 25 E (3 miles East of SR 49, Kemil Road at US 12)

Chesterton 46304

- ❑ Phone: (219) 926-1952 www.in.gov/dnr/parklake/2980.htm
- ❑ Hours: Dawn to dusk. Nature Center: 9:30am-4:30pm.
- ❑ Admission: $7-$12.00 per vehicle.
- ❑ Note: Offers swimming, hiking, beach house, concessions, camping, playground equipment and picnic shelters. Nature center has year-round program for all ages

The Nature Center offers a 12 minute video about dunes and surrounding plant life that is helpful to watch before exploring.

The largest "live" dune, Mt. Baldy ("live" means it still moves as wind lifts grains of sand & drops them) is guaranteed to make your mouth drop and your eyes open wide. It's a thrill to climb quickly to the top (123 ft.) and let the dune slide you down to the water's edge. (Note to Parents: be ready for an aerobic workout!). On a windy day, place a beach toy on the sand and watch a mini-dune form behind it! On a windy day you can also hear the sand "sing" under your feet – it's true!

Another site to visit (esp. during special events) is the Bailly Homestead and Chellberg Farm. Visit the home of one of Porter County's earliest settlers, French-Canadian voyageur and fur trader Joseph Bailly. Nearby is an early 20th century 80-acre working farm established in 1874 by Swedish immigrants Anders and Johanna Kjellberg, who emigrated from Sweden in 1863. (Both properties on Mineral Springs Road, between U.S. Highways 12 and 20, Porter. 219-926-7561, extension 225).

DEEP RIVER WATERPARK

9001 E. US 30 (off I-65), Crown Point 46307

❑   Phone: (219) 947-7349 www.deepriverwaterpark.com

❑   Hours: Daily 10:00am-5:00pm (Memorial Day Weekend - Labor Day, excluding the last two Monday-Fridays in August). Central Time.

❑   Admission: $40-$42 General, $4 discount for child (under 46") and senior. Reduced rates for special night tubing and off-peak weekdays. Free tubes for tube rides.

❑   Note: Treats and café. Coolers are allowed, too.

There is a lot to do at this Waterpark including a wave pool, lazy river, Tube and Body slides, and many adventurous waterslides like "The Storm" tunnel tube ride. Among the places to play: the Paddlers' Play Area, which offers low-key fun for children; and The Dragon, a wild water slide that can send "sliders" down at speeds up to 35 mph. Bringing a big group? Consider playing Water Wars, an interactive water challenge game.

ADAMS MILL

4595 County Road S 75 E (1/2 mile east of town on Rte. 500 south & 75E - road to mill)

Cutler 46920

❑   Phone: (765) 463-7893

    www.adams-mill.org

❑   Hours: Weekends 1:00-5:00pm (mid April- mid-October), 11:00am-5:00pm for events (usually held once per month).

❑   Admission: $5.00 family, $2.00 adult, $1.00 child.

A grist mill with hundreds of pioneer life antiques displayed. A display of "Americana". Most of the original mill equipment is running. Monthly events are the best time to visit…especially the Treasure Hunts.

WABASH AND ERIE CANAL PARK CENTER
1030 N. Washington St. (off US 421), **Delphi** 46923

❑ Phone: (765) 564-2870

www.wabashanderiecanal.org

❑ Hours: Monday-Saturday 1:00-4:00pm (warm months only for canal rides) April – December.

❑ Admission: $10.00 (age 13+), $5.00 (age 12 and under). $17.00 combo includes canal boat ride, museum and home. Child $5.00

❑ Educators: Teachers Packet-
http://docs.wixstatic.com/ugd/934a4e_c530f6704d054734b19ab0 5646cdc76a.pdf

In the 1800s, the nation's longest canal, the Wabash and Erie Canal, ran from Toledo, Ohio, to Evansville. Although these waterways have given way to superhighways, this city hasn't forgotten the impact of the canal on American history. The Wabash, which had long been a native thoroughfare servicing the inhabitants of the area, became alive with water traffic and related businesses. Items exported from this area were grain, logs, pork, and whiskey. Numbered among the imports were coffee, salt, manufactured goods, and settlers. Most of the workers were Irish immigrants.

Volunteers have brought to life the Wabash and Erie Canal Park Interpretive Center. The facility's museum galleries include more than 60 exhibits. Everything from dinosaur remains to scaled-down models of a section of the canal and bridge. Outside, they have a Canal Playboat.

True historians can hike, bike or walk the 1850s canal, a seven-mile trail system. Better yet, experience a 35-minute floating trip on The Delphi, a replica 19th century canal boat. Tour guides share adventures and stories of everyday life as it was 150 years ago on the Wabash & Erie Canal.

FAIR OAKS FARMS

856 North 600 East (off I-65 North)

Fair Oaks 47943

❏ Phone: (219) 394-2025   www.fofarms.com
❏ Hours: Cowfe and shop opens early. Dining until 9pm. Central Time.
❏ Tours: Daily 10am-5pm. Admission to Dairy Adventures/Mooville/Crop Adventure/Pig Adventure is $25 for all. Mooville alone $13.00.
❏ Note: The center is FREE to browse but plan on a café purchase – famous grilled cheese and chocolate milk!

Want to make milk more exciting to your kids? Take them to the Fair Oaks Dairy Adventure. It's a chance to learn about the dairy industry through interactive displays, videos, and a tour of a modern dairy farm. The "Grass to the Glass" video highlights: Farming & Crop Harvest, Feeding, Calf Taking its First Steps, Milking & Herd Management, Milk Safety & Transportation, Processing & Bottling, Production of Ice Cream, Cheese, Yogurt & Other Dairy Products, and Enjoying Dairy Products.

Mooville (summer only): Catch some major air on the massive Dairy Air jumping pillow. Hang tight as you climb to Udder Heights, a 25-foot milk bottle-shaped climbing wall. Find your way through the String Cheese Maze. The little ones can enjoy a ride on the MooChoo train, or race around the track on Holstein Haulers. Kids young and old can experience the Cowabunga Bungee Experience-you are strapped in with bungee chords and sprung high into the air!

WinField Crop Adventure takes you underneath a farmer's fields, where you will see and touch the world of bugs, roots, seeds and soil. The Pig Adventure is all about pigs and pork.

Board a bus and tour a farm to see the feeding, milking and care of dairy cows. This is one of the largest dairy farms in the country. About 80 calves are born at this farm every day.

WOOD'S HISTORIC GRIST MILL

9410 Old Lincoln Highway (in Deep River County Park)

Hobart 46342

❑   Phone: (219) 947-1958   https://lakecountyparks.com/151/Deep-River-County-Park

❑   Hours: Daily 10:00am-5:00pm (May-October)

❑   Admission: FREE (child 12 and under). $0.50 adult.

❑   Note: General Store - old fashioned wooden floors, jars of candy and sundries.

Restored late 1800's mill designed to expose you to the process of a gristmill and pioneer life. Daily demonstrations of grinding corn into meal and the sale of the stone ground cornmeal occur in the mill. Rag rugs are often being made on an antique loom, and the replica General Store beckons visitors back to a time long past. The first floor is where the raw grain is ground by large stones. The other two floors are displays of period settings. Also take a peek in the 1830's sawmill.

STARKE COUNTY HISTORICAL MUSEUM

1520 S Heaton Street (2 blocks west of US 35)

Knox 46534

❑   Phone: (574) 772-7242   https://www.starkehistory.org/

❑   Hours: Friday 10:00am-4:00pm.

❑   Admission: FREE

❑   Note: Annual events include the July 4th Ice Cream Social and a Christmas Open House.

Starke County Historical Museum is quartered in the home of banker, businessman, twice-elected Governor of Indiana, Henry F. Schricker. The museum holds three floors of historical memorabilia including agricultural, military items, clothing, decorative items, toys, a schoolroom and the Schricker Room containing the family's personal collections.

HESSTON STEAM MUSEUM

313 Kintzele Road (I-94 or I80/90 on SR 39 to east on County. Rd. 1000N)

Michigan City 46360

- ❑ Phone: (219) 872-5055, www.hesston.org
- ❑ Hours: Weekends Noon-5:00pm (Memorial Day-Labor Day & October). Sunday only (September). CDT
- ❑ Admission: FREE to grounds and museum, except on Labor Day weekend. Passenger ride tickets: $5.00-$9.00.

¼ scale and 1/8 scale steam trains give rides around 155 wooded acres, climbing a grade, crossing several dams, running alongside ponds or dams and depots.

Also, steam crane, sawmill, traction engine and threshing machines, power plant and more. Visit The Depot Store for a wide variety of steam related items including tee and sweatshirts, "Thomas the Tank Engine"® toys and much more. They also put in an old-fashioned soda fountain and ice cream parlor.

OLD LIGHTHOUSE MUSEUM

Heisman Harbor Road

Michigan City 46360

- ❑ Phone: (219) 872-6133   https://www.mchistorical.org/
- ❑ Hours: Wednesday-Sunday 1:00-4:00p. Closed November-March. CT
- ❑ Admission: $10.00 general, FREE child (14 and younger) and military.

An original 1858 lighthouse filled with displays of recreated keeper's house, lake lore, ship wrecks, and maritime history. Take the cat walk out to the only operational lighthouse in Indiana. Learn how the lighthouse keeper and his/her family (the most famous keeper was a woman) lived and worked.

WASHINGTON PARK ZOO

115 Lake Shore Drive (On the Lake in Washington Park. Take US 421/Franklin Street North through Michigan City until it dead ends)

Michigan City 46360

- ❑ Phone: (219) 873-1510
  www.facebook.com/washingtonparkzoo
- ❑ Hours: Daily 10:00am-4:00pm (April-October). Open later in the summer.
- ❑ Admission: $8.00-$10.00 (age 3+).

A 1928 zoo laid out on the side of a wooded sand dune. One of the oldest and largest zoos with a petting area (near the entrance), children's castle, feline house, turtle pond, bobcat/prairie dog display and monkey island. You also can see the Michigan shoreline and Chicago skyline from the observation tower.

INDIANA BEACH AMUSEMENT

5224 East Indiana Beach Road (I-65 to US 24)

Monticello 47960

- ❑ Phone: (574) 583-4141, www.indianabeach.com
- ❑ Hours: Summer hours 11:00am-11:00pm. (mid May-Labor Day)
- ❑ Admission: Waterpark and rides passes combo are $31.99-$41.99. Seniors: $21.99.
- ❑ Note: Camp Resort. Free Parking.

The 1400 acre lake with sandy beach provides a day full of entertainment. Popular amusements are the "Hoosier Hurricane" or "Corn Ball Express" rides along with Kiddieland, an arcade, mini-golf, and mini-train rides. Indiana Beach thrills visitors with a newer ride: Air Crow. Climb aboard to fly over the waters of Lake Shafer. Riders can swing themselves higher for an even more breathtaking experience.

Browse or eat at the Boardwalk and then take the plunge on the "Big Flush" waterslide in the WaterPark. To relax, try a ride on the "Shafer Queen" paddle wheel boat.

HOOSIER VALLEY RAILROAD MUSEUM

507 Mulberry Street

North Jordan 46366

❑   Phone: www.hoosiervalley.org
❑   Tours: Saturdays & Sundays - 11am, 1pm and 3pm departures.
    Saturdays Diesel 10am, Noon, and 2pm. CDT (May thru
    October, plus Santa Train in December). Ride is 40 to 45-minutes
    / 10-miles "roundtrip". $14.00 Adult. $10.00 Youth (age 6-15).
❑   Admission: Museum is FREE. Open 9am-4pm ride days.
❑   Notes: Take in the quiet scenery along the North Judson Erie
    Trail. About 9 miles of the trail is open to the public between the
    trailhead at HVRM in North Judson and U.S. 35 near Bass Lake.

Tucked away in this picturesque rural community, HVRM
has become the destination of people who want to
experience the post-World War II railroading.

Ride behind a vintage diesel locomotive in various sytles of
railroad cabooses, and an open-air sightseeing car. Travel
through the rural farm country of Starke and southern
LaPorte counties. Flowers, butterflies, wildlife and lots of
Indiana crops visible from the train. Roundtrip - North
Judson to English Lake / Kankakee River Bridge.

PORTER COUNTY OLD JAIL MUSEUM

20 Indiana Avenue

Valparaiso 46383

❑   Phone: (219) 465-3595   https://www.pocomuse.org/museum
❑   Hours: Tuesday-Sunday 11:00am-4:00pm
❑   Admission: FREE

The Sheriff's home is an Italianate brick building that
contains rooms of period furniture. The jail is a two-story
structure leading to the Sheriff's home.

See an exhibit on Wild West Bronco John (Buffalo Bill's
partner) and dress from the Inaugural Ball of Abe Lincoln.

GUSE CHRISTMAS TREE FARM

6177 West 1450 South

Wanatah 46390

- ❏ Phone: (219) 733-9346 www.gusechristmastrees.com
- ❏ Hours: Daily 8:00am-4:00pm (Thanksgiving-Christmas Eve)
- ❏ Admission: FREE
- ❏ Tours: By appointment. 45 minutes long. (mid-November to mid-December)

This is a 3rd and 4th generation year round business raising Christmas trees. 125 acres of trees show how different trees grow, how Christmas wreaths are made, and the operations it takes to make the finest trees. Come and cut or dig a Douglas, Fraiser Fir, Scotch, White Pine or Blue Spruce. Enjoy horse-drawn wagon rides and Santa-visits every weekend. Petting zoo and pony rides. Warm up with hot cocoa.

WHOAZONE

1443 Park Service RD

Whiting (Whihala Beach) 46394

- ❏ Phone: 219-234-2615 https://whoa.zone/whiting/
- ❏ Hours: 11am – 6pm daily, weather permitting (mid June - mid August).
- ❏ Admission: Single Splash (50 minutes, ages 7+ & 45"+) $23.00 per person. Sessions start on the hour.

WhoaZone is an inflatable playground, the largest one in the Midwest! The obstacle course is provided by Wibit - the leader in the industry of water fun. Whihala Beach is the area's best kept secret featuring a beautiful white sandy beach on Lake Michigan, lots of parking, restrooms, concessions and a safe place for summer family fun!

MASCOT HALL OF FAME

1851 Front Street

Whiting 46394

❑   Phone: (219) 354-8814   https://mascothalloffame.com/
❑   Hours: Open Tuesday-Thursday 10AM - 3PM, Friday 10AM - 7PM, Saturday 10AM - 5PM
❑   Admission: Adults and Children Ages 2+: $10.00.

The Mascot Hall of Fame is a hall of fame for United States sports mascots. The mission is to honor mascot performers, performances, and programs that have positively affected their communities. Guests experience exhibits such as the "Department of Furry Arts", the "Science of Silliness Lab", and the "Phuzzical Education Department". Not only is everything calling out to be touched, played with, read, or messed with, but it is educational and easy enough for younger audiences to figure out.

TIPPECANOE RIVER STATE PARK

4200 North US 35

Winamac 46996

❑   Phone: (574) 946-3213
     www.in.gov/dnr/parklake/2965.htm
❑   Admission: $7-$9.00 per vehicle.

This park is most used for the bridle trails and excellent canoeing. During the summer when you want to swim, just take your current gate or campground receipt to Bass Lake State Beach for free admission. Warning: mosquitoes can be very annoying at times during the season. Repellent is advised! Also camping, hiking, fishing and seasonal programs (like cross-country skiing in winter).

Chapter 7
South East Area - (SE)

Our Favorites...

* Falls of the Ohio - Clarksville

* Zimmerman Art Glass - Corydon

* Squire Boone Caverns & Village - Mauckport

* State Historic Sites & State Parks

"Artists in Action"... Zimmerman Art Glass

DEAM LAKE STATE RECREATION AREA
1217 Deam Lake Road, SR 60
Borden 47106

❑   Phone: (812) 246-5421

> www.in.gov/dnr/forestry/4825.htm

Deam Lake is forest property designed for recreational activities. Activities include fishing, boating, swimming, camping, picnicking, hiking, swimming, rowboat rentals, hiking trails and a Nature Center. The 194-acre lake was constructed in 1965 and was named in honor of Charles Deam, Indiana's first state forester. Deam is best known for his book, Trees of Indiana, a comprehensive study of trees throughout the state.

BROWNSTOWN SPEEDWAY
Hwy. 250, one mile southeast of town (Jackson County Fairgrounds), **Brownstown** 47220

❑   Phone: (812) 358-5332

> www.brownstownspeedway.com

❑   Hours: Racing Saturdays at 7:00pm (March-October).

Stock car races including Late Models, Modifieds, Street Stocks, and Bombers. Admission charged.

JACKSON-WASHINGTON STATE FOREST
1278 East SR 250 (located 2.5 miles southeast of Brownstown on St. Rd. 250), **Brownstown** 47220

❑   Phone: (812) 358-2160

> www.in.gov/dnr/forestry/4820.htm

This part of the state contains unique topography known as the "knobs" region, and affords scenic views from Skyline Drive and some breathtaking hiking trails. Archery Range, Basketball and Volleyball Courts, Bridle Trails.

CHARLESTOWN STATE PARK

PO Box 38 (west of SR 62)

Charlestown 47111

- ❑   Phone: (812) 256-5600
  www.in.gov/dnr/parklake/2986.htm
- ❑   Hours: Open year-round.
- ❑   Admission: $5.00-$7.00/vehicle.

Devonian fossils, Bird Watchers, Hiking (rugged and moderate trails available); Formerly part of the Indiana Ammunition Plant - so much of the ground is unspoiled; Camping area on site.

DERBY DINNER PLAYHOUSE

525 Marriott Drive

Clarksville 47129

- ❑   Phone: (812) 288-2632 or (812) 288-8281 tickets
  www.derbydinner.com
- ❑   Hours: Performances Tuesday-Sunday. Doors open at 6:00pm for Buffet Dinner - Show starts at 8:00pm. Matinees - Wednesday & Sunday. Doors open at 11:45am - Show at 1:30pm.
- ❑   Admission: Tickets: $45.00-$51.00. $6.00 for Children's Theatre Student Matinee.

A dinner theater in the round featuring top-notch performances of Broadway productions served after a buffet dinner. Shows run for approximately 6 weeks and special shows are offered periodically. Children's theatre programs offered of seasonal themes or cartoon favorites (breakfast and lunch shows for these performances).

FALLS OF THE OHIO STATE PARK

201 West Riverside Drive (I – 65 Exit 0, follow signs)

Clarksville 47129

❑ Phone: (812) 280-9970, www.fallsoftheohio.org
❑ Hours: Center open Monday-Saturday 9:00am-5:00pm, Sunday 1:00-5:00pm. Park open daily dawn to dusk. Closed Thanksgiving and Christmas
❑ Admission: Interpretive Center - $9.00 adult, $7.00 child (5-11). $2.00 parking fee.
❑ Tours: Guided tours of fossil beds May-October (EDST).
❑ Note: Boat Launch Ramp/Ohio River, Hiking Trails, Picnicking, Bird Watching, Fishing, Gift Shop, and Ohio River and Coral Reef Aquariums. Educators: Activity Sheets: www.fallsoftheohio.org/FallsStudentPrograms.html

The "Age of Fish" coral reef fossil beds are among the largest exposed Devonian fossil beds in the world. The park features a spectacular visitor center overlooking the fossil beds containing an exhibit and video presentation.

While fossil collecting is prohibited, visitors are free to explore – we could identify corals, sponges, sea shells and snails. The months of August through October are the most accessible as the river is at its lowest level. Tip: It was suggested to splash water on a colony area and they will "jump out" showing exquisite detail.

The Interpretive Center features a full size mammoth skeleton, plus there are exhibits on geology, history and cultural development of the Falls of the Ohio.

CORYDON CAPITOL STATE HISTORIC SITE

202 East Walnut Street (I-64 exit 105 to downtown), **Corydon** 47112

- ❑ Phone: (812) 738-4890
  https://www.indianamuseum.org/historic-sites/corydon-capitol/
- ❑ Hours: Tuesday-Saturday 9:00am-5:00pm, Sunday 1:00-5:00pm.
  Timed, indoor tours are available Wednesday through Sunday at
  10 a.m., 12 p.m., 2 p.m. and 4 p.m.. Closed Thanksgiving,
  Christmas Eve, Christmas Day, New Year's Day and Easter.
  Limited winter hours.
- ❑ Admission: $8.00 adult, $7.00 senior (60+), $5.00 youth (3-17).
- ❑ Note: Visitor center and gift shop. Several Special events are also
  held to celebrate Indiana's heritage.

This Site includes the restored 1816 limestone state capitol
building, Governor's residence, and first state office building
among other landmarks in the area. Limestone was hauled
from nearby quarries to erect the 40 foot square walls, and
poplar and walnut logs were cut from virgin forests from the
ceiling and roof supports. In June of 1816, 43 delegates met
in Corydon to draft the first state constitution. Much of their
work was done under the shade of a huge elm tree. The trunk
of the tree, now known as the "Constitution Elm," is still
standing. The State Historic Site recounts Indiana's early
days of statehood.

HARRISON CRAWFORD STATE FOREST / WYANDOTTE COMPLEX STATE FOREST

7240 Old Forest Road SW (bordering the Ohio River)

Corydon 47112

- ❑ Phone: (812) 738-8232.
  www.in.gov/dnr/forestry/4826.htm

Timber is the key resource consideration in the management
and use of Indiana's State Forests. The timber is continually
evaluated to determine management needs such as
harvesting, planting, thinning or timber stand improvement.
Openings created by timber harvesting also increase wildlife

habitat. These openings guarantee stable and healthy populations of both game and non-game species. Recreation here includes fishing, canoeing, a campground, an Olympic size swimming pool, a forestry interpretive center, several picnic areas, and hiking and horse trails.

ZIMMERMAN ART GLASS COMPANY

300 East Chestnut Street (I-64 exit 105 to SR 135 South to SR 62 to Mulberry (right turn)

Corydon 47112

- ❏ Phone: (812) 738-2206
  https://www.facebook.com/ZimmermanArtGlassBusiness/
- ❏ Hours: Monday-Friday 10:00am-5:00pm, Saturday 10:00am-4:00pm.
- ❏ Admission: FREE
- ❏ Tours: 30 minute demos, Tuesday-Friday only 10:00am-1:00pm or 2:00-4:00pm.
- ❏ Note: Recently produced and signed art glass pieces available on site for purchase – you just have to wait until they finish the piece they're working on. Educators: teacher unit study materials are on their home page.

Generations-old and world-renowned glass artisans make hand-blown glass paperweights, lamps, bowls and bottles. Two brothers work in a workshop in an workspace so small that you can stand close to the artist. Watch as they get a glob of premixed colored molten glass and, by constantly twirling it on a long stick, begin to use old tools to shape the "glob" into their signature "flower". After a few cycles of heating/shaping/cooling the flower, they let it "twirl cool" to make the final paperweight with a blossomed flower inside. You have to see this remarkable process! Our group was speechless and mesmerized to the point that we didn't even ask questions.

SQUIRE BOONE CAVERNS AND VILLAGE

100 Squire Boone Road SW (I – 64 exit 105. Watch for signs - some pretty tricky)

Corydon (Mauckport) 47142

❏   Phone: (502) 425-CAVE or (812) 732-4382
    www.squireboonecaverns.com &
    www.squireboonecavernsziplines.com
❏   Hours: Daily 9:00am – 5:00pm. (Memorial Day to Labor Day).
    Pre-scheduled the rest of the year between 10:00am – 4:00pm
    every two hours. Closed Thanksgiving, Christmas Eve,
    Christmas, New Years.
❏   Admission: Caverns: $25.00 adult, $23.00 senior (60+), $15.00
    child (4-11). Zipline: $59.00 (April-November) $3.00 parking fee
    per vehicle in summer. Internet coupons.
❏   Tours: Summers - Last one hour. Every 30 minutes. Spring and
    Fall Months, January and February: Tours depart at 10 am, 12
    pm, 2 pm and 4 pm, seven days a week. In case of inclement
    weather, please call ahead.
❏   Ziplines run by reservation only. Must be at least 7 yrs old.
    Group packages include hayrides and bonfires.
❏   Note: Gem mining (fossils and gems), soap and candlemaking,
    petting zoo and playground (Summer only, $7.00). Caverns are a
    constant 54 degrees year round. A light jacket is suggested.

Explore the same caverns that Squire and Daniel Boone discovered in 1790 as Squire was out searching for his older brother, Daniel who had been captured by hostile Indians. Walk past stalactites, stalagmites, blind and albino crayfish, underground streams and waterfalls, dams, and the foundation stone carved by Squire himself. It's all very quiet. Squire's life was spared when he hid in the caverns from a band of pursuing Indians – he is even buried in his beloved cave. Buy a spelunking explorer hat with light for the kids to use while they tour. Then they have a great souvenir that was actually used at the site. Onto the foundation stones of his mill, Squire Boone carved this inscription: "My God my life hath much befriended, I'll praise Him till my days are ended."

The *Squire Boone Caverns Zipline* Adventures canopy course includes: •6 Canopy zip lines •1 Swinging Suspension Bridge •Comfortable and secure full body harness •Views of the Caverns and Village along with acres of forests. •Ends at Squire Boone Village making it easy to begin your next adventure!

Built by Squire Boone in the early 1800's, the mill area has been restored and is again grinding grain just as it did nearly two centuries ago. You can watch as the 18 foot wheel, powered by water flowing from the caverns, turns the 1,000 pound grinding stones. The miller also demonstrates how cornmeal and grits are sifted out of the ground corn. Cornmeal can be purchased at the Grist Mill.

CLARK STATE FOREST

PO Box 119 (Located on U.S. Highway 31, 10 miles south of Scottsburg or one mile north of Henryville just off I-65)

Henryville 47126

❏   Phone: (812) 294-4306

     www.in.gov/dnr/forestry/4827.htm

❏   Note: Camping, short Hiking Trails, Seven Fishing Lakes, and Bridle Trails.

Clark State Forest, established in 1903, is the oldest state forest in Indiana. Much of this land was originally part of Clark's Grant, lands provided by a clause in the Virginia Cession of Claims to the Northwest Territory on December 20, 1783.

HOWARD STEAMBOAT MUSEUM

1101 East Market Street (I-65, exit 0)

Jeffersonville 47130

- ❑ Phone: (812) 283-3728 or www.howardsteamboatmuseum.org
- ❑ Hours: Tuesday-Saturday 10:00am-3:00pm, Sunday Noon-3:00pm. Closed major holidays.
- ❑ Admission: $10.00 adult, $8.00 senior (65+), $6.00 students (age 6 thru college).

The museum has a large collection of steamboat models, tools, artifacts, etc. from the Great Steamboat Era. The 1894 Victorian Mansion also has many of the original furnishings and family possessions. The mansion was built by the Howard's, premier steamboat builders. Kids love seeing all the stained glass windows, especially when the sun shines through.

LAWRENCEBURG SPEEDWAY

351 East Eads Parkway (I-275 exit SR 50, Dearborn County Fairgrounds)

Lawrenceburg 47025

- ❑ Phone: (812) 539-4700
  https://www.lawrenceburgspeedway.com/
- ❑ Hours: Gates Open 5:00pm, Practice laps 6:20pm, Racing 7:15pm. (May-September)
- ❑ Admission: $17.00 adult, $8.00 youth (7-12). Pit Passes - $35.00. Prices may vary with sanctioned shows/special events.

1/4 Mile High Banked Clay Oval with weekly racing divisions in Non-wing Sprints, Modifieds and Pro Stocks.

PERFECT NORTH SLOPES

19640 SR 1 (From I-275 take the US 50 Exit 16, follow ski area
signs north on Indiana Route 1)

Lawrenceburg 47025

❏ Phone: (812) 537-3754 www.perfectnorth.com

❏ Hours: Weekdays 9:30am-9:30pm, Weekends 9:30am-3:00am
(December to mid-March).

❏ Admission: Flex Tickets (all day) $79.00. Season Passes $100.00
and up. Children 6 & under - ski free with a paying adult or if
taking a lesson. Active Duty Military & family will receive
discount with valid ID.

With 70 acres of tree-lined trails and wide open slopes, they
have skiing for all abilities. They offer ski school, night
skiing, equipment rental and purchase.

CLIFTY FALLS STATE PARK

1501 Green Road (off SR 62 or 56)

Madison 47250

❏ Phone: (812) 265-4135 Inn or (812) 273-8885 park
www.in.gov/dnr/parklake/2985.htm

❏ Admission: $7.00-$9.00 per vehicle.

The name Clifty Falls paints a beautiful picture in your
mind. Winter and spring hiking trails show the falls at their
best while the splendor of the creek and canyon offer
exciting scenery year-round.

In historic Madison, tour the mansion of frontier banker
James F.D. Lanier and enjoy the drive along the beautiful
Ohio River. Plan a park visit during one of the community's
special events such as the Madison Chautauqua Art Festival
or Regatta hydroplane boat race.

Clifty Inn has accommodations and a Restaurant. At the Inn
is a seasonal Swimming/Pool with waterslide, tennis & other
games. Camping and a Nature Center are here too.

JEFFERSON COUNTY MUSEUM AND RAILROAD STATION DEPOT

615 West First Street (and Mill Streets on Ohio River)

Madison 47250

- ❏ Phone: (812) 265-2335, www.jchshc.org
- ❏ Hours: Tuesday-Friday 10:00am-3:30pm. (May-October). Weekdays only. (November-April), except closed mid-December – February.
- ❏ Admission: $5.00 general admission.

The Pioneer exhibit is a re-created stone house, typical of early rural dwellings. In it is a varied collection of early farming and domestic artifacts. The Steamboat exhibit explains the important role the Ohio River has played in the history of the area. The Civil War exhibit chronicles the famous raid of Confederate General John Hunt Morgan through the county, and explores the roles of soldiers in the Civil War. The Victorian Parlor exhibit highlights period furniture, clothing, artwork, and artifacts, all with a local history. The Octagonal Railroad Station displays history of first Indiana railroad. A restored Caboose sits nearby.

Stop over to Dr. William Hutchings' Office (on West 3rd) or The Sullivan House (on West 2nd) for more historical county insight. Located in a historic stone house on the grounds of Madison State Hospital, the new Gatehouse Museum features photos, exhibits and artifacts telling the history of the hospital since its opening in 1910; and tracing the changes over the years in the care of mental patients.

LANIER MANSION STATE HISTORIC SITE

601 West First Street

Madison 47250

- ❑ Phone: (812) 265-3526
  https://www.indianamuseum.org/historic-sites/lanier-mansion/
- ❑ Hours: Wednesday-Sunday 10:00am-5:00pm. The site is closed on Easter, Thanksgiving, Christmas Eve, Christmas Day and New Year's Day, and Columbus Day, Veterans Day.
- ❑ Tours: Timed, indoor tours are available Wednesday through Sunday at 10 a.m., 12 p.m., 2 p.m. and 4 p.m.
- ❑ Admission: $12.00 adult, $10.00 senior (60+), $8.00 child (3-17)

On the banks of the Ohio River stands a stately mansion built for James Franklin Doughty Lanier - a man who, at one time, saved Indiana from financial ruin. With national expansion booming, Lanier's talents as a financier brought him great fortune. The Greek Revival home is especially noted for its staircases. Especially fun for special events like Lanier Civil War Days in June, Spooky Mansion in October or Spirit of Christmas Past in December.

THE FLOYD COUNTY LIBRARY CULTURAL ARTS CENTER

201 East Spring Street (Eastbound on I-64, take exit #123)

New Albany 47150

- ❑ Phone: (812) 944-7336, https://floydlibrary.org/cultural-arts-center/
- ❑ Hours: Monday-Thursday 10am-7pm, Friday-Saturday 10am-5pm.
- ❑ Admission: FREE, donations accepted.

The contemporary art gallery and local history museum has permanent and traveling exhibits. This is the home of the famous "Yenowine Folk Art Dioramas - a hand-carved animated diorama depicting scenes from early Indiana.

CULBERTSON MANSION STATE HISTORIC PARK

914 East Main Street (off I-64), **New Albany** 47150

- ❑ Phone: (812) 244-9600
  https://www.indianamuseum.org/historic-sites/culbertson-mansion/
- ❑ Hours: Wednesday-Sunday 10:00am-5:00pm. Weekdays only in Winter. Closed each January. Special events each October and December.
- ❑ Tours: Timed, indoor tours are available Wednesday through Sunday at 10 a.m., 12 p.m., 2 p.m. and 4 p.m.
- ❑ Admission: $12 adult, $10 senior (60+), $8 child (3-17).

A Victorian mansion that stands as an impressive tribute to one of Indiana's leading merchants and philanthropists, William Culbertson. The Culbertson Mansion represents the lifestyles of the Victorian fortune-makers as well as the lifestyles of the servant staffs. Visitors may view the grand parlors, dining rooms, bedrooms, kitchen and laundry room of the 25 room mansion.

OHIO COUNTY HISTORICAL MUSEUM

212 South Walnut Street

Rising Sun 47040

- ❑ Phone: (812) 438-4915
  www.ohiocountyhistory.org
- ❑ Hours: Monday-Friday 10:00am-4:00pm.Saturday & Sunday Noon-4:00pm.
- ❑ Admission: $1.00-$2.50 (age 13+), FREE child (under 12).

Home of "Hoosier Boy" a 1900 racing boat with the fastest time between Louisville and Cincinnati. The museum has an original Auto Harp - first coin operated music player.

HARDY LAKE STATE RESERVOIR

4171 East Harrod Road

Scottsburg 47170

❑ Phone: (812) 794-3800.

www.in.gov/dnr/parklake/2958.htm

2,178 acres and a 741-acre lake provide facilities like: Archery Range, Sport Courts, Horseshoe Pits, Boating, Camping, Cultural Arts Programs, Fishing / Ice Fishing, Hiking Trails, Interpretive / Recreational Programs, Picnicking / Shelter houses, Playgrounds, Rental-Rowboat, Swimming / Beach, and Water-skiing.

PIGEON ROOST STATE HISTORIC SITE

(5 miles south of Scottsburg on US 31)

Scottsburg 47170

❑ Phone: (812) 265-3526

www.in.gov/history/markers/12.htm

❑ Hours: Open dawn to dusk.

❑ Admission: FREE, donations accepted.

The first of several conflicts in the Indiana Territory during the War of 1812 occurred at the small settlement of Pigeon Roost, a few miles south of present-day Scottsburg.

The site is a 44 foot limestone monument memorializing 24 settlers killed during an 1812 raid. The immediate result of the Pigeon Roost conflict was the effect it had on settlers. Fearing further attacks, communities surrounding Pigeon Roost moved into forts and blockhouses. Settlers planned more militia raids on Native American settlements across the Indiana Territory. Skirmishes between settlers and tribes continued until the Treaty of Ghent was signed in 1814 ending the War of 1812.

STARVE HOLLOW STATE RECREATION AREA

4345 South CR 275 West, **Vallonia** 47281

❏   Phone: (812) 358-3464.

www.in.gov/dnr/forestry/4819.htm

When it was first constructed in 1938, Starve Hollow Lake was the largest body of water, in wide area, in Indiana.

The lake now covers 145 acres. Although no longer Indiana's largest lake, Starve Hollow Lake offers some of the best fishing in southern Indiana. Volleyball, Softball & Basketball, Camping and Swimming, too.

VERSAILLES STATE PARK

Box 205, US 50

Versailles 47042

❏   Phone: (812) 689-6424

www.in.gov/dnr/parklake/2963.htm

❏   Admission: $5.00-$7.00 per vehicle.

Relax while fishing on the 230-acre lake where you can rent a paddleboat, rowboat or canoe. Bring your bicycle and pedal the nearby 27-mile Hoosier Hills Bicycle Route. Also Bridle Trails, Swimming / Pool and waterslide.

SUGGESTED LODGING AND DINING

SCHIMPFF'S CONFECTIONERY - **Jeffersonville**. 347 Spring Street. http://www.schimpffs.com/ Phone: (812) 283-8367. Famous for their cinnamon red hots. Schimpff's is a fourth generation, family-owned business that features a soda fountain, original tin ceiling, antique memorabilia and tasty candies. Lunch counter.

Chapter 8
South West Area - (SW)

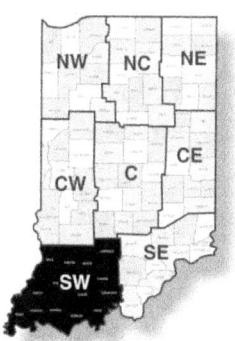

Our Favorites...

* Angel Mounds Historic Site - Evansville

* Evansville Museum of Arts, History, and Science - Evansville

* Log Inn - Haubstadt

* Lincoln Boyhood Home Attraction - Lincoln City

* Grouseland - Vincennes

* Indiana Territory Capitol Village - Vincennes

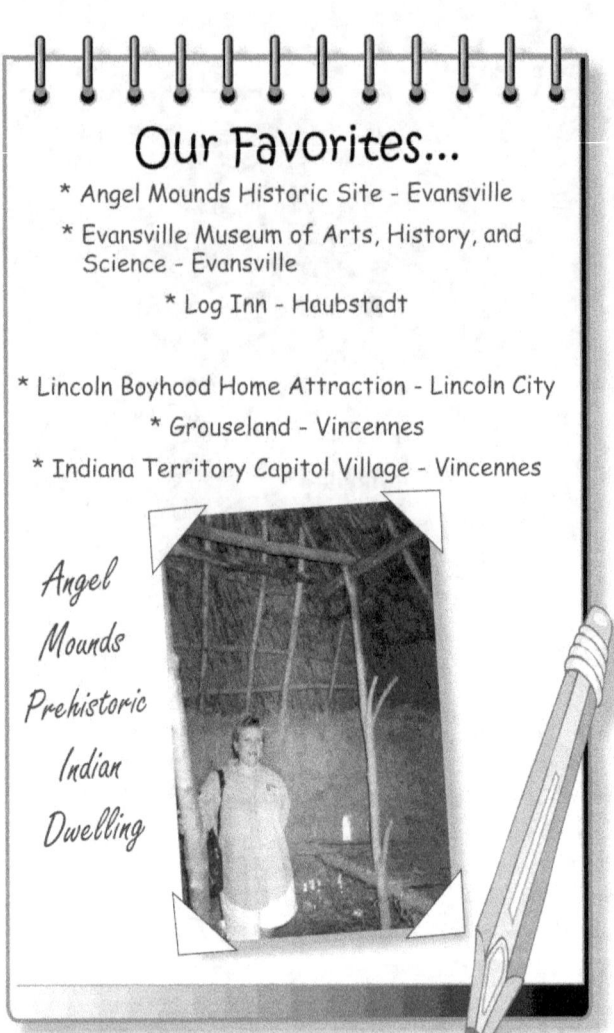

Angel Mounds Prehistoric Indian Dwelling

BLUESPRING CAVERNS PARK

1459 Bluespring Caverns Road (US 50 and SR 37 on CR 450 South)

Bedford 47421

- ❏ Phone: (812) 279-9471
  www.bluespringcaverns.com
- ❏ Hours: Daily 9:00am-4:00pm. (April-October). Extended summer and weekend hours. EST.
- ❏ Admission: $24.00 adult, $12.00 child (15 & younger). The tour is not recommended for infants and very young children. The walk into the Caverns to tour boats and back to the surface is 800 feet and is a fairly steep ramp.
- ❏ Tours: Tours hourly or more often on Saturdays & Sundays and during the summer.
- ❏ Note: Always a 52 degree constant temperature – a light jacket recommended. Myst'ry River Gemstone Mine – prospect for your own gemstones. "Overnight Adventures" for organized youth groups.

Years ago the White River cut into small cracks in limestone rock and dissolved it forming cave passages. As glaciers moved into the area they brought debris of soil and rock that were deposited. In the 1940's, a large pond on a farm disappeared overnight to reveal the entrance to the cave. The Myst'ry River tour boat glides along the quiet waters into the heart of a subterranean natural world. The guide will point out unusual formations and the interesting albino blind fish and crawfish that live in darkness.

HOOSIER STATE FOREST

811 Constitution Avenue (Brownstown Ranger District)

Bedford 47421

❑ Phone: (812) 275-5987 (Brownstown) and (812) 547-7051 (Tell City Ranger), https://www.fs.usda.gov/hoosier

Situated in the rolling hills of south central Indiana, the Hoosier hides its geologic landscapes beneath a canopy of hickory and oak. A little exploration reveals a landscape of underground rivers, caves, sinkholes, box canyons, limestone bluffs, and narrow ridges. The most popular spots are:

❑ <u>WATCHABLE WILDLIFE SITES</u> - Buzzard Roost Overlook is located approximately two miles north of Magnet.

❑ <u>CHARLES C. DEAM WILDERNESS</u> - Indiana's only Congressionally designated wilderness area has 13,000 acres providing for solitude and a remote experience.

❑ <u>HICKORY RIDGE LOOKOUT TOWER</u> - Constructed by the CCC in 1939.

❑ <u>PIONEER MOTHERS MEMORIAL FOREST</u> - An 88 acre virgin old-growth forest and archaeological site. Explore virgin forest of ancient oaks and 130-foot walnut trees with 42-inch diameters.

❑ <u>LICK CREEK SETTLEMENT</u> - site of a 1815-1900 African American settlement.

❑ <u>HEMLOCK CLIFFS</u> - a box-shaped canyon with sandstone formations, seasonal water falls and rock shelters. And, of course, the canyon's cool climate is perfect for hemlock -- these tall evergreens with short needles and small cones simply thrive in this environment and so will you. Hemlock Cliffs is located west of Highway 37 about two miles north of Interstate 64.

❑ <u>RICKENBAUGH HOUSE</u> - A stone house built in 1874, used as a local post office and church meeting house.

For updates, visit our website: www.KidsLoveTravel.com

- SUNDANCE LAKE - a 5 acre lake named for a Native American spiritual dance held annually near the site.
- CLOVER LICK BARRENS - Shallow soils and rock outcrops are found in these prairie-like, fire-dependant ecosystems which have many rare species.
- WESLEY CHAPEL GULF - This National Natural Landmark is an 8 acre collapsed sinkhole with a floor which provides a window to the underground river system.
- BUFFALO TRACE - an historic pathway used by migrating buffalo from the Falls of the Ohio River near Louisville to Vincennes where they crossed into the Illinois prairie.
- TIPSHAW LAKE BEACH - This beach offers a combination of sand and sun, or shady grass-covered hillside.

The Ohio River and the forest's four lakes offer a little something for everyone, including swimming, waterfowl viewing, canoeing, boating, and fishing for catfish and bass.

PATOKA LAKE STATE RESERVOIR
RR 1, Birdseye 47513

- Phone: (812) 685-2464 or (812) 547-7028
  www.in.gov/dnr/parklake/2953.htm

Archery range, Frisbee Golf Course, Solar Heated Visitors Center (illustrated displays on wildlife, history, birds of prey, solar energy and the viewing of a live bald eagle are all part of the Center's Raptor Education Program), house-boating, water-skiing, swimming, and fishing. Large campgrounds, launching ramps, marina, paved biking trails and a large supervised beach and swimming (Memorial to Labor Day). Lodging is available at cozy cabins and rustic chalets near or on the lake.

WESSELMAN WOODS NATURE PRESERVE

551 North Boeke Road (I-164 to SR 66)

Evansville 47711

- ❏ Phone: (812) 479-0771   https://wesselmanwoods.org/
- ❏ Hours: Open Tuesday through Saturday 9 AM - 5 PM. Trail access is free from 7:30-9 AM on Tuesday through Friday. Sunday 12 - 5 PM. CLOSED on Mondays. Wesselman Woods closes at 4 PM during our winter season (November-March). Closed Mondays & Thanksgivingtime, Xmastime, New Years time.
- ❏ Admission: Adults - $5.00, Children (ages 3 – 12 years old) - $3.00.

An ancient forest with 200 acres of bottomland hardwood forest, fields and ponds. The Nature Center has trail maps, lists of wildflowers, birds and trees to look for and brochures covering maple sugaring, pioneer skills and forestry.

The preserve - where you can also find a section of the historic Wabash & Erie Canal - is home to myriad wildflowers, deer, birds, and a host of other wildlife. Stop by the Nature Center and leaf through exhibits and a wildlife observation room. The Center hosts Animal Encounters most Sunday afternoons at 2:00pm. Often naturalists lead free short, family-friendly hikes with hands-on activities to engage the kids. Nature playscapes use natural landscapes, natural vegetation and materials in a creative and interactive way for unstructured child play and exploration.

EVANSVILLE MUSEUM OF ARTS, HISTORY AND SCIENCE

411 SE Riverside Drive (downtown in Sunset Park, at the corner of Cherry St and Riverside Dr. (Veterans Memorial Parkway becomes Riverside Drive one block from the Museum)

Evansville 47713

❑ Phone: (812) 425-2406, https://evansvillemuseum.org/

❑ Hours: Thursday-Saturday 11am-5pm, Sunday Noon-5:00pm. CDT. Open summer Wednesdays.

❑ Admission: $12.00 adult, $8.00 child (4-17). EMTRAC admission $2.00 adult. Children under 12 are free if accompanied by an adult. Admission to Koch Immersive Theater $7.00 adult, $5.00 child (3-12).

❑ Note: Museum Shop. Collection of artwork from the 16th century to the present and an Anthropology gallery on the two upper levels. Koch Planetarium has "themed" programs weekly.

Explore prehistoric, Native American and Main Street (late 1800's) History. Old-style tools they used, types of buildings they lived in, and what the kids played with back then. What was it like to live in a river city at the turn of the 20th Century? Take a walk through Rivertown, USA for an historic look at early Evansville. Using the ceramic sculpture, The Kingdom Builders, students compare similarities in the early cultures of Egypt and Mexico. An exhibit on Abraham Lincoln, the early Indiana years, is here too.

The Science Center for school-aged and pre-school kids has hands-on exhibits dealing with lasers, optical illusions, gravity and spatial relationships - all very applicable to everyday situations. Many "theme" exhibits focus on subjects like weather or the "art of science".

The Transportation Center (outside) – "EMTRAC" focuses on modes of early transport - dugout canals, steam boats, autos, and steam locomotives.

ANGEL MOUNDS STATE HISTORIC SITE
8215 Pollack Avenue (I -164 to Highway 662, Covert Avenue Exit)

Evansville 47715

- ❑ Phone: (812) 853-3956,
     https://www.indianamuseum.org/historic-sites/angel-mounds/
- ❑ Hours: Wednesday-Sunday 10:00am-5:00pm (mid-March to mid-December)
- ❑ Admission: $7.00 adult, $6.00 senior (60+), $4.00 child (3-12).
- ❑ Note: Interpretive Center. Nature preserve. Picnic Area.

Located on the banks of the Ohio River, this is a well-preserved prehistoric Indian settlement of the Mississippians who planted corn, hunted and fished for food in the area for over 250 years. The Indians had 1000 - 3000 people populate the area. 11 earthen mounds served as elevated buildings until mysteriously abandoned.

The site also includes reconstructed winter houses, a round house, summer houses, a stockade and a temple that formed a village within the mounds. Learn about home and fortress construction - do you know what "waffle" and "daub" mean? -- (twigs woven between logs, then plastered with clay). The Middle-Mississippi tribe were known for their pottery and animal-shaped toys made from clay with added crushed mussel shells (used as a tempering agent). A popular kids game called "chunky" is played by throwing spears at small rolling stone discs. The closest spear wins. The earthen, thatched living huts had heating and air-conditioning - how?

CHILDREN'S MUSEUM OF EVANSVILLE (CMOE)
22 SE Fifth Street (I-64 exit 25A to Hwy 41S to IN 62W to MLK exit. Follow signs), **Evansville 47708**

- ❑ Phone: (812) 464-cmoe   www.cmoekids.org
- ❑ Hours: Tuesday-Thursday 9am-4pm, Friday-Saturday 9am-5pm, Sunday Noon-5pm.

❑ Admission: $15.00 (18 months and older)

A place for kids ages 3-12 and their adults where children "play to learn" and adults "learn to play". It hosts four main galleries, plus a multimedia theater entitled the 'Freedom Gallery.' 'Work Smart' focuses on engineering skill development and the freedom to build and create. 'Live Well' provides inquiry into our bodies and promotes the freedom to make choices. Quack Factory is a kooky water play area and Speak Loud is full of costumes, makeup, creativity and drama.

MESKER PARK ZOO AND BOTANIC GARDEN

2421 Bement Avenue (off SR 66, Mesker Park)

Evansville 47720

❑ Phone: (812) 428-0715   https://meskerparkzoo.com/

❑ Hours: Daily 9:00am-4:00pm.

❑ Admission: $10.00-$11.00 (ages 3+).

❑ Educators: Activity books and Scavenger Hunts:
https://meskerparkzoo.com/teachers

The rolling hills of this 70 some acres are home to approximately 600 animals. Indiana's largest zoo includes a petting zoo, zoo train, Lake Victoria paddle boat rides, Discovery Center rain forest and Jungle Cafe. Resident monkeys live in the center of a lake in a concrete replica of Christopher Columbus' Santa Maria.

The zoo is divided into the African Panorama, Tropical Americas, Asian Valley, Lemur Forest, and North America forest - including lions and a tiger, birds of all feathers, monkeys and lemurs, gazelle and giraffe, kangaroos and kudus, leopards and a warthog, zebras & zebus. Favorites to look for: Mechi the rhino and the camel with two humps!

LOG INN

Old State Rd (RR 2, I-64 to US 41 East), **Evansville (Haubstadt)**
47639

- ❑ Phone: (812) 867-3216 or www.theloginn.net
- ❑ Hours: Tuesday-Thursday 4:00-8:00pm, Friday-Saturday 4:00-8:30pm. Closed in January.
- ❑ Admission: Around $15 adult, $8.00 child for Family Style Dinners.

Built in 1825 as a Noon Day Stage Coach Stop and Trading Post. Dine in the same original Log Room that Abraham Lincoln stopped at in November, 1844, enroute back from visiting his mother's grave. It was part of his campaign speaking tour. Officially recognized as the oldest restaurant in Indiana, authentic 1-foot thick logs surround you as you eat their wonderful fried chicken meals. Take time to read the articles on the walls while you wait for dinner. Dinners served by a la carte menu or family style.

PIKE STATE FOREST

6583 East SR 364 (off State Road 364, four miles east of State Road 61)

Ferdinand 47532

- ❑ Phone: (812) 367-1524
  www.in.gov/dnr/forestry/4823.htm

Topography at Pike State Forest varies from hilly uplands to the low bottomlands of the Patoka River. Because of the diversity of sites, a wide variety of plant and animal life make their homes at Pike. Several recreational opportunities are available at Pike State Forest, including hunting, horseback riding, picnicking, bird watching and hiking.

FRENCH LICK SPRINGS RESORT

8670 West State Road 56

French Lick 47432

❑ Phone: (800) 457-4042 reservations or (812) 936-9300

www.frenchlick.com

Tour the century old grand hotel with reasonable resort accommodations and kid-friendly activities like: Archery, Badminton, Basketball, Bike Rental, Bingo, Board Games, Boating (Patoka Lake), Bowling, Croquet, Fishing (Patoka Lake), Golf, Horseback Riding, Miniature Golf, Playground, Kids Club with childcare and planned activities, Playground, Nature Hikes, Pony Rides, Rec Center (arcade), Skiing (Paoli Peaks), Surrey Rides, Swimming (indoor/outdoor), Tennis (indoor /outdoor), Train Rides (IN Railway Museum), Trolley Rides and Volleyball. Some activities are available during season (May - October) only. Availability of some activities is subject to weather conditions. Many activities charge separate fees. Parents can play golf or go to the spa springs treatments while kids are at the KidsFest.

FRENCH LICK SCENIC RAILWAY

SR 56, 1 Monon Street (SR 37 to Paoli, go West on Hwy 56/150 to French Lick), **French Lick** 47432

❑ Phone: (812) 936-2405 or (800) 74-TRAIN

www.frenchlickscenicrailway.org

❑ Hours: Weekends and Holidays 10:00am, 1:00pm & 4:00 pm. (April-October). Tuesday at 1pm summers.

❑ Admission: $25.00 adult, $200.00 child (2-11) for family rides. Regular tours each weekend at 1pm are $32.00 per person open air car, $38.00 per person 1ˢᵗ class table.

❑ Tours: 1 hour, 40 mile train trip.

❑ Note: Train Robbery Rides one weekend per month including Memorial Day, July 4th and Labor Day weekends. Gift Shop and snacks.

The museum displays diesel and steam locomotives, a rare railway Post Office car and a 1951 dining car.

The Springs Valley Electric Trolley (shortest trolley line in the world) carries passengers for a little ride for a little fee ($1.00-2.00). Catch a weekend or summer Tuesday afternoon train where you pass by Larry Bird's boyhood home, a log cabin, Parson's Falls and the coolest part – the long, completely pitch dark tunnel. We all clapped once we made it through! The area's history is related by uniformed crew members - many who have personal stories to tell.

COLONEL WILLIAM JONES STATE HISTORIC SITE

Rte. 1, Box 600 (one mile west of US 231 on Boone Street)

Gentryville 47537

❑   Phone: (812) 937-2802
www.abrahamlincolnonline.org/lincoln/sites/jones.htm
❑   Hours: Wednesday-Saturday 9:00am-5:00pm, Sunday 1:00-5:00pm (mid-March to mid-December).
❑   Admission: FREE. Donations accepted.
❑   Note: Situated on 100 acres of forest, the site offers a self-guiding nature trail, picnic area and a restored log barn.

This carefully restored 1834 Federal-design home of the merchant employer of Abraham Lincoln offers a unique look at the early development of Indiana and the life of Colonel William Jones, who was also a politician, farmer and soldier. The home includes guided tours, themed talks, and exhibits.

DUBOIS COUNTY MUSEUM

1103 Main Street (Gramelspacher-Gutzweiler Bldg.)

Jasper 47546

❑   Phone: (812) 634-7733 or (800) 968-4578
www.duboiscountymuseum.org
❑   Hours: Tuesday-Friday 10:00am-2:00pm, Saturday 10am-4pm, Sunday 1-4pm. EST

❑   Admission: FREE. Donations accepted.

The Museum traces the region's dynamic history from the Ice Age to the present. Archaic Indians roamed the forests and glens that once blanketed this land. They were followed by the Piankshaw Indians, who preceded the Scots-Irish settlers. An overwhelming migration of Germans arrived in the Mid-Nineteenth Century.

Visit a log cabin home of early settlers, stop by the Mercantile for some fashion tips, look at a wild game safari display, a tremendous model train display, and also discover the death rituals of the early people.

INDIANA BASEBALL HALL OF FAME

1436 Leopold Street, Hwy. 162 & College Avenue (Campus of Vincennes Univ. - Jasper, Ruxer Student Center)

Jasper 47546

❑   Phone: (812) 482-2262

www.indbaseballhalloffame.org

❑   Hours: Daily 11:00am-3:00pm (summer), Thursday-Sunday rest of year. Closed legal holidays.

❑   Admission: $4.00 adult, $2.00 senior (60+), $3.00 child (5-12).

The sponsoring body of the hall of fame is the Indiana High School Baseball Coaches Association, IHSBCA, which has served the baseball coaches of Indiana since 1971. The first inductions were in July 1979 and there are currently 91 inductees in the hall of fame in four categories: pro-player, coach-manager (high school, college, pro), contributor and veteran.

LINCOLN BOYHOOD NATIONAL MEMORIAL

3027 East South Street, SR 162 (I-64 exit 57, US 231 south thru
Dale to Gentryville.Then, east on SR 162 for 2 miles), **Lincoln City**
47552

- ❑   Phone: (812) 937-4541, https://www.nps.gov/libo/
- ❑   Hours: Visitor Center Wednesday-Sunday 9:00am-3:00pm (daily
      summer hours). Closed for lunch between Noon-1pm. The farm
      is staffed from Memorial Day wkend thru early August. CDT.
- ❑   Admission: Admission to the park is FREE.
- ❑   Note: Picnic Shelter. Over 2 miles of hiking trails and roads in
      the park to walk with your pet. Educators: Wonderful Lincoln
      Unit Studies - www.nps.gov/libo/forteachers/index.htm

The Visitor Center has a museum with film "Forging
Greatness: Lincoln in Indiana" (from age 7-21 years) - young
Abe Lincoln.

The Cabin site is a working pioneer farmstead with animals
and crops where Abraham used to split rails, plant and plow
or milk cows. Rangers dressed in period clothing perform a
variety of activities typical of daily life in the 1820s. See his
mother's grave (she died of "milksick" when he was 9 years
old).

We learned that "milksick" is a disease caused by poisonous
milk produced by cows that eat snakeroot (if pastures are
dry, cows migrate to forest areas where poisonous plants
grow).

Walk on the Boyhood Nature Trails - the same trails that a
young Abraham would have walked alone in thought years
ago.

LINCOLN STATE PARK

Lincoln State Park Amphitheatre (I-64, Exit 57 to US 231 South)

Lincoln City 47552

❑   Phone: (812) 937-4710 (park) or
    www.in.gov/dnr/parklake/2979.htm
❑   Hours: Wednesday-Monday 10am-2pm (May thru mid-August).
    Weekends only (mid-August thru October).
❑   Admission: $7.00-$9.00 per vehicle.

Lincoln State Park is a scenic 1,747-acre park established in 1932 as a memorial to Nancy Hanks Lincoln. Recreational facilities include Lake Lincoln, lakeside shelter house, boat rental building, nature center, cabins, picnic areas, shelters and trails, plus Class A and primitive camp sites.

CAVE COUNTRY CANOES - BLUE RIVER

PO Box 217, 112 Main Street

Marengo 47140

❑   Phone: (812) 365-2705

www.cavecountrycanoes.com

❑   Season: (April-October)

❑   Admission: Begin at $48.00 per person.

❑   Tours: Half day (2-4 hours) and Full day (4-7 hours) trips, guided. All rates include paddle, lifejacket, map and transportation.

Two bases to serve you... Milltown & Leavenworth. Enjoy canoes, kayaks & shuttle service on the Blue River ... the most spring fed of all Indiana's streams. The many springs account for the aqua-blue color of the river, leading to the name "The Blue". In many areas limestone bluffs, dotted with cave entrances, tower above the river attesting to the fact that "The Blue" flows through the heart of Indiana's Cave Country. The river valley is noted for its abundant wildlife, natural beauty, and excellent fishing.

MARENGO CAVE

400 East State Road 64 (I – 64 to SR 66 and SR 64 west)

Marengo 47140

❑   Phone: (812) 365-2705, www.marengocave.com

❑   Hours: Daily 9:00 am-5:00 pm. Closed Christmas and Thanksgiving Day. EST.

❑   Admission: $21.95-$24.95 adult, $12.95-$14.95 child (4–12). Combine tours and save $9.00-$16.00 per person.

❑   Tours: Leave every 30 minutes

❑   Note: Hungry Grotto Snack Shop. Cave Springs Mining Company – gemstone mining – Daily, (April-October). Climbing Tower. Canoe trips, trail rides. Camping.

Tours include:

❑ CRYSTAL PALACE TOUR – 40 minutes, world famous "Crystal Palace" cave room with dramatic lighting presentation. Mountain rooms and massive deposits.

❑ DRIPSTONE TRAIL TOUR – One hour and 10 minutes. Known for soda straw formations, slender and intricate "dripping" deposits. Includes "Pulpit Rock", "Music Hall" and "Penny Ceiling".

SPRING MILL STATE PARK

3333 St Rte 60 E (SR 37 to SR 60 East), **Mitchell** 47446

❑ Phone: (812) 849-4129

   www.in.gov/dnr/parklake/2968.htm

❑ Admission: $7.00-$9.00 per vehicle.

Lots to do and see here. Beginning with the Spring Mill Inn (812) 849-4081 - Accommodations and Restaurant.

Tour the restored *Pioneer Village* including a gristmill, lime kiln, sawmill, hat shop, post office, apothecary and boot shop. (open daily 9am-5pm May thru mid-October)

Plan to take a boat ride into Twin Caves (tour times are assigned daily, they are seasonal). *Twin Caves Boat Tour* is open Daily from Memorial Day Weekend thru mid-August, 9:00 a.m. to 5:00 p.m. Open Weekends from mid-August thru mid-October, 9:00 a.m. to 5:00 p.m.

Tours run on the half-hour. Only same-day reservations are accepted and they must be made in-person at the Twin Caves shack. Cost is $3/person; no credit cards. Children under age 3 are not allowed on the tour.

The underground world of the park is opened up to visitors on this unique cave tour. Guides pull the boats thru a stream passage while highlighting cave formations and searching for cave animals (the endangered blind cavefish is a common sighting).

Grissom Memorial honors Hoosier astronaut "Gus" Grissom, one of seven Mercury astronauts and America's second man in space (space capsule and video of space exploration).

Other facilities include: Indoor Swimming/Pool, Tennis & other games, Camping, Cultural Arts Programs, Fishing / Ice Fishing, Hiking Trails, Nature Center (open daily 10am-5pm March thru October), and a Saddle Barn.

GASTHOF AMISH VILLAGE
City Road 650 East (off US 150)
Montgomery 47558

❑   Phone: (812) 486-3977 or (812) 486–2600
www.gasthofamishvillage.com
❑   Hours: Daily Lunch/Dinner.

Tours by buggy pass a harness shop, quilt and craft shop, general store and candy factory. The restaurant, built of Indiana oak and poplar, was framed by Amish carpenters with simple joints and pegs. Amish cooking. Many "Amish" or "Harvest" Festivals are held at site year-round.

HARMONIE STATE PARK
3451 Harmonie State Park Road (Off CR 69 - on the banks of the Wabash)
New Harmony 47631

❑   Phone: (812) 682-4821. www.in.gov/dnr/parklake/2981.htm
❑   Admission: $7.00-$9.00 per vehicle.

Located "on the banks of the Wabash," 25 miles northwest of Evansville, this park has a beautiful swimming pool, shady picnic areas, and ravines. Easy to Moderate Trails for walking, biking and nature hikes will lure you for a visit. They also have cabins and a Nature Center.

PAOLI PEAKS SKI & SNOWBOARD RESORT

2798 W. CR 25 S

Paoli 47454

❑ Phone: (812) 723-4696, www.paolipeaks.com

❑ Hours: Monday-Thursday 10:00am-9:30pm, Friday 10:00am-10:00pm and Friday & Saturday Midnight-6:00am, Saturday 9:00am-10:00pm, Sunday 9:00am-9:30pm. See website for special holiday hours.

❑ Admission: Every activity involves a fee. Many packages available. Go online for best information.

On the Slopes there is a natural hill with 300 ft. vertical drop. Average grade: 10%-15%. Terrain: 25% beginner, 55% intermediate, 10% advanced, 10% expert park. 1 quad chair, 3 triple chairs, 1 beginner double chair, 3 surface tows.

❑ SKI LODGE - 45,000 square ft. day lodge with self service restaurant & pizzeria, rentals and shops and ticket sales.

❑ LODGING & ACCOMMODATIONS - Condominiums next to the slopes, B&B's, cabins, motels, resort hotels.

❑ KID'S SNOW CAMP - All day supervision includes four hours of instruction and lunch. ages 4-12.

❑ KIDS FUN PARK - Kids can learn & improve their skills while enjoying time in the Kids' Fun Park. Our expanded Snow Park for youngsters features brightly colored foam figures to ski around, a snow tunnel and the cool "Wonder Carpet", an 80 foot moving sidewalk on the snow.

LINCOLN PIONEER VILLAGE & MUSEUM

416 Main Street (Rockport City Park, at west end of Main)

Rockport 47635

❑ Phone: (812) 649-4215
http://lincolnpioneervillage.com
❑ Hours: Monday-Saturday 9am-3pm, Sunday Noon-4pm (May-October). .
❑ Admission: $3.00-$5.00

The Lincoln Pioneer Village Museum houses hundreds of fascinating artifacts from the area's historic past including a hutch made by Abraham Lincoln's father, Thomas.

Located next to the museum is the historic Lincoln Pioneer Village, consisting of cabins that are replicas from the Lincoln era in Spencer County (cabins may be seen on weekends or, by appointment- including the law office, schoolhouse, church, store and typical cabin homes).

HOLIDAY WORLD THEME PARK AND SPLASHIN' SAFARI

452 East Christmas Blvd. (7 miles South of I-64, exit 63, Highway 162), **Santa Claus** 47579

❑ Phone: (877) GO-FAMILY
www.holidayworld.com
❑ Hours: Holiday World opens 9:30am. Splashin' Safari 10:30 am. CDT. Closing varies by season. (May to mid-October)
❑ Admission: General range $49.99 (age 4+).
❑ Notes: Season passes and 2-day passes save money. Charge cards taken.

HOLIDAY WORLD is consistently rated as one of the cleanest amusement parks in the mid-West. We rate this park high for families mostly because it has great atmosphere and caters to kids ages 2-15. Everyone loves the free parking, free sunscreen and especially the free soda (self-serve stations located throughout the park). Their pizza is very good, too. Included in admission are Live shows (country, pop, high dive); Raging Rapids whitewater rafting ride; Spin-dry on Revolution; The Raven; The Legend or the Howlert coasters; Frightful Falls log flume ride; Costumed characters roam about in Holidog's Funtown; and Banshee six story weightlessness ride. Santa appears daily-look for him mostly in Rudolph's Ranch Kiddie Park. We liked all the shows, the Swing ride and every ride in the waterpark.

SPLASHIN' SAFARI is where Certified lifeguards oversee fun areas like: Monsoon Lagoon - a 12 level interactive area with water effects, body slides and the GIANT bucket; Congo River tube float; Zoombabwe - the largest waterslide in the world; Watubee whitewater ride; Speed slide; two wave pools (one small, one huge); covered slide; and Crocodile Isle - scaled-down pool and slides for the younger set. Jungle Racer, the first 10-lane racing slide complex ever built, is a water slide so you're guaranteed to cool off even if you're in hot competition with other sliders! The Jungle Jets area features 163 water elements, such as geysers and drenching spray arches. Nearly every water ride comes with tubes, which is so nice for adults to "cushion" the ride, and makes it easier to manage with kids.

LAKE RUDOLPH CAMPGROUND & RV RESORT

78 North Holiday Blvd (right next door to Holiday World)

Santa Claus 47579

❏   Phone: (877) YES RUDY or www.lakerudolph.com
❏   Notes: If you're not cooking breakfast over the open firs, try St. Nicks Restaurant in Santa's Lodge. The have a great breakfast buffet.

The campground offers a free shuttle service to the amusement park plus discount tickets. For $79 to $119 per night you can overnight amongst other families "roughing it". Actually, this is quite comfortable accommodations. We'd recommend camping with your own gear or renting an RV. Either way, you can cook and eat each evening under the stars. If you're not busy site-seeing, ride your bike, walk or rent a golf cart visiting the camp store, play in the game room, a splash pad, paddleboat, play mini-golf, or swim at one of two pools. They have a fishing pond too. Their numberous bathhouses provide modern bathrooms and showers for campers.

Rudolph's Christmas Cabins also include flat screen TVs, electric fireplaces, large decks and gas grills, and are even available to stay during the Christmas season.

If you have time, walk the 2/3 mile trail called the Trail of 12 Stones. Each of the twelve stone markers details a different phase of Lincoln's life. Each stone is from the actual foundation of a site Abe visited in his life. Pretty cool!

MARTIN STATE FOREST

PO Box 599 (4 miles east of Shoals, Indiana on U.S. Highway 50)

Shoals 47581

❑   Phone: (812) 247-3491.
     www.in.gov/dnr/forestry/4822.htm

Martin State Forest offers a variety of educational opportunities through its woodland management trail and arboretum. The forest features rugged hills, deep woods and long hiking trails.

The Arboretum Trail (.25 mile easy) is an informal arboretum (a place for the study and exhibition of trees) was established in an existing wooded area. The collection currently contains about 60 different species identified by signs along the trail.

The goal of the Martin State Forest Hoosier Woodland Arboretum is to offer a representation of the common woodland trees of Indiana. Martin State Forest offers 7 miles of mountain bike trails.

TELL CITY PRETZELS

402 Jackson Street

Tell City (Jasper-the Pretzel Experience) 47546

❑   Phone: (812) 548-4499   https://tellcitypretzel.com/

❑   Store Hours: 8am – 5pm Monday through Friday

What's been around for over 100 years and still has the same delicious, crunchy taste as the first day they were made? Handmade pretzels from Tell City, Indiana. Tell City Pretzels has a long history of pretzel making that started with a recipe established by Casper Gloor from Switzerland. His top secret recipe is still used at the factory today and even though it's not available to the public, visitors to the factory can watch the pretzels being made the original way – by hand twisting them. What are they known for: their crunch.

FLOOD WALL MURAL AT SUNSET PARK

Sunset Park, Ohio River (Washington & 7th Street)

Tell City 47586

❑   Phone: (812) 547-7933

        www.facebook.com/SunsetParkFloodwallMural

Sunset park contains a painted mural on the flood wall.

It was done in sections and took 3 years to paint. It is a rendition of early days of Perry County. Each building, boat and person has historical significance. Each of ten panels has a theme such as manufacturing, lifestyle (residences), mills, banks, merchants and steamboats.

GEORGE ROGERS CLARK NATIONAL HISTORIC PARK

401 South 2nd Street (downtown, just blocks from waterfront)

Vincennes 47591

- ❏ Phone: (812) 882-1776   https://www.nps.gov/gero/
- ❏ Hours: Daily 9:00am-5:00pm. Eastern Time Zone.
- ❏ Admission: FREE.

The site of a little-known, but extremely important, battle that occurred during the Revolutionary War. On February 25, 1779 Virginian George Rogers Clark, with his small army of American frontiersmen and French inhabitants, captured Fort Sackville from the British. Clark's victory aided the United States in laying claim to the vast region that later became the Old Northwest Territory.

Today a massive granite-and-marble memorial, more than 80 feet high, stands on the location of Fort Sackville and pays tribute to Clark and his men. Inside are Clark's words carved into Indiana limestone "Great things have been effected by a few men well conducted." Within the visitor center view a 30-minute movie "Long Knives" and look over a few mannequin exhibits. Costumed living history programs are randomly offered.

GROUSELAND

3 West Scott Street (Downtown at Park and Scott Streets)

Vincennes 47591

- ❏ Phone: (812) 882-2096   https://grouseland.org/
- ❏ Hours: Tuesday-Saturday Noon-4:00pm.
- ❏ Admission: $7.00 adult, $5.00 child (age 6+)
- ❏ Tours: Ring the doorbell and a guide will escort you in.

The Home of William Henry Harrison, the first Governor of the Indiana Territory and later the 9th President of the United States. He died in office 31 days after his inauguration - some say unnecessarily due to blood letting.

For updates, visit our website: www.KidsLoveTravel.com

The dining room has a bullet hole in the window shutter where someone tried to shoot Harrison (they missed!). As you walk from upstairs down to the warming kitchen, you'll see a cutaway of original flooring used in the home. The layers of clay and straw underneath wood provided insulation and noise protection (Harrison didn't want servants to eavesdrop). Stories for the kids include the "giant travel chest" and a Mother's apron needle used for more than sewing. Mr. Harrison is best known for his campaign against Tecumseh.The Treaty of Grouseland was signed at his home.

INDIANA MILITARY MUSEUM

715 S 6th Street

Vincennes 47591

❏   Phone: (812) 882-8668 or (800) 886-6443
    www.indymilitary.com
❏   Hours: Daily 10:00am-4:00pm. Winter hours vary. Its outdoor
    static displays may be viewed from 8:00am-5:00pm daily.
❏   Admission: $8.00 adult, $5.00 student (5-17).
❏   Tours: Guided tours only by arrangement.

Military history from the Civil War to Desert Storm. Outdoors - tanks, artillery, helicopters. Indoors - uniforms, flags, relics from battlefields, captured enemy souvenirs, World War II toys and homefront items.

INDIANA TERRITORY CAPITOL VILLAGE

1 West Harrison Street (from US 41, enter town at Sixth St. Head south to College Ave. Turn right. Follow signs)

Vincennes 47591

❏   Phone: (812) 882-7472
    https://www.indianamuseum.org/historic-sites/vincennes/
❏   Hours: Wednesday-Sunday 10:00am-2:00pm.
❏   Admission: $8.00 adult, $7.00 senior (60+), $5.00 child (3-12).
❏   Tours: Begin at Log Cabin Visitor's Center
❏

❑   Note: Videotape of Vincennes' history in the Visitor's Center. OLD FRENCH HOUSE AND INDIAN MUSEUM is nearby and exhibits pioneer life including influences of early inhabitants, American Indian tribes.

Start at the oldest major government building in the Midwest - the Indiana Territory Capitol Building. Then, stop in for a demonstration of old-fashioned printing presses at the Elias Stout Print Shop...a replica print shop where they first printed the Law of the Territory and the first Territory newspaper, "The Indiana Gazette." Learn where we got the phrase, "UPPER CASE or capital letters" and "mind your P's and Q's". Lastly, step inside Maurice Thompson's birthplace where the author of "Alice of Old Vincennes" (a best-selling romance novel) was born. It features frame construction, instead of logs, and a cast iron stove in place of a drafty fireplace - both modern for the time.

This is a volunteer-lead village and, if you plan it right, you'll come during peak times when all the "villagers" are bustling about their chores or reenacting major Territory events.

Chapter 9

Seasonal & Special Events

*Note: **Pioneer Encampments** are listed in the back of this section.*

JANUARY

BROWN COUNTY WINTER HIKE

C – Nashville, Brown County State Park. https://www.browncounty.com/ The event features two separate trails for enjoying wildlife, peace and solitude…a day to toss off those winter blahs. Exercise your body and mind with knowledgeable naturalists located throughout the hike to offer interpretive info and answer questions about the park. A special Hiker's Buffet Luncheon – featuring hot, hearty, home-cooked food- will be available at the Abe Martin Lodge. State Park fee. (Saturday after New Years)

FEBRUARY / MARCH

MAPLE SYRUP FESTIVALS

Learn how maple syrup is made from tree tapping to evaporator demonstrations. Taste sampling of food with syrup like pancakes and kettle popcorn. Pioneer music and games.

- ❑ **CW – Terre Haute**. Prairie Creek Park Log Cabin. (812) 462-3391. FREE (month long in February thru early March)
- ❑ **NC – Wakarusa**. Downtown. (574) 862-2714. Parade, chain saw carving, pedal-pull contests. FREE (last week of April)
- ❑ **NE – LaGrange**. Maplewood Nature Center. (260) 463-4022. Admission. (third weekend in March)
- ❑ **SE – Salem**. Sugarbush Farm. (812) 967-4491 or www.lmsugarbush.com . FREE
- ❑ **SW - Evansville**. Wesselman Woods Nature Preserve. (812) 479-0771. Admission. (early March weekend)

MAY

500 FESTIVALS, THE

(Activities to celebrate the Indy 500 Race), www.500festival.com .

❑   **C – Anderson.** ANDERSON LITTLE 500 FESTIVAL & RACE. Various locations. (765) 640-2437. Big wheel race, concert, fireworks, sprint car race. Admission. (week before Memorial Day)

❑   **C – Indianapolis.** KIDS DAY. Monument Circle. (800) 638-4296. The city's largest outdoor festival for children with Big Wheel races (ages 2-5), carnival, arts and crafts, prizes. No Admission. except for racers (Sat before Memorial Day wkend)

❑   **C – Indianapolis.** 500 FESTIVAL COMMUNITY DAY. Motor Speedway. (317) 614-6124. Lap the track in your own vehicle. See Pit Row, Gasoline Alley, and the Tower Terrace. Driver's and mechanic's autographs. Admission. (Thursday before race)

❑   **C – Indianapolis.** 500 FESTIVAL PARADE. Downtown. (800) 638-4296. Drivers, floats, marching bands, celebrities. Admission for reserved seating. (Noon the day before race)

❑   **C – Indianapolis.** INDIANAPOLIS 500 MILE RACE. Motor Speedway. (800) 638-4296. The world's largest one-day sporting event. Admission. (Memorial Day)

WHISTLE STOP DAYS

NW – Hesston. Hesston Steam Museum. www.hesston.org. Ride three steam railroads, visit operating steam sawmill, steam crane, steam power plant and more. FREE, train rides have fee. (Memorial Day Weekend)

HARRISON COUNTY POPCORN FESTIVAL

SE   –   Corydon.   Courthouse   Square. https://www.facebook.com/HarrisonCoPopcornFestival/   Celebrate the county's popcorn industry (and the home of popular Cousin Willie's Popcorn). Parade, popcorn demos and contests, popcorn-related foods and some star entertainer. FREE. (mid-month weekend in May)

WINGS OVER MUSCATATUCK

SE – Seymour. Muscatatuck Nat'l Wildlife Refuge, I-65 & US 50. www.facebook.com/MuscatatuckNWR   Indiana's   International Migratory Bird Festival – celebrating birds and the natural environment. Field trips, guided bird walks, bird crafts, bird photography, bird calling, tracking, puppet shows. Adm field trips. (second long wkend in May)

JUNE

STRAWBERRY FESTIVALS

Sample strawberry treats like fresh strawberry shortcakes and strawberry ice cream or sundaes. Entertainment. Kids activities.

- ❏   **CE – Metamora**. Along the canal. www.metamora.com . FREE. (first weekend in June)
- ❏   **CW – Crawfordsville**. Historic Lane Place. www.crawfordsville.org . FREE. (second weekend in June)
- ❏   **CW – Terre Haute**. Downtown. (812) 232-8880. Admission. (third Saturday in June)
- ❏   **NC – Wabash**. Historic Downtown. Very Berry Strawberry Fest. (260) 563-0975. FREE. (second Saturday in June)

BILL MONROE MEMORIAL BEAN BLOSSOM BLUEGRASS FESTIVAL

C – Bean Blossom.   Bluegrass   Hall   or   Fame   Museum. https://billmonroemusicpark.com/ The   longest   continuously   running bluegrass festival in the world, held outdoors with six days of the best in bluegrass, featuring 25 bands, band contest, artist workshops, crafts, children's workshops, pickin' and jammin', food. Camping, cabin rentals, fishing and hiking trails. Admission. (second or third week in June)

WILBUR WRIGHT FESTIVAL

CE – Millville.   Wilbur Wright Birthplace & Museum, CR 750 East. https://wwbirthplace.com/events. Home tours, outdoor life-size replica of the 1903 Wright Flyer, live entertainment, flea market, car show, sky divers, kite flying, remote-controlled planes, tours, beans and cornbread. Pork chop dinner Saturday. Admission. (third weekend in June)

TASTE OF TIPPECANOE

CW – Lafayette. Downtown, Riehle Plaza. www.tasteoftippecanoe.org .Outdoor festival featuring six stages with live entertainment, 30 local restaurant vendors, Kid's Taste area, fireworks. Admission. (third Saturday in June)

GLASS FESTIVAL

NC – Greentown. Downtown. www.greentownglass.org . This town's birthday features tours of the glass factory (see rare Chocolate Glass – invented here), re-enactors, historical displays, children's activities, food, music, and historical play. FREE. (second weekend in June)

EGG FESTIVAL

NC– Mentone. Menser Park. https://mentoneeggcity.com/egg-festival/ The egg basket of the Midwest features the incredible edible egg in a parade, tractor pull, crafts, variety show. FREE. (first weekend in June)

ROUND BARN FESTIVAL

NC – Rochester. Downtown, Main Street. https://www.fultoncountyhistory.org/ Bus tour of round barns and one-room school, bed races, rodeo, parade, kiddy races, wall rock climbing, food, entertainment, games. FREE. (second weekend in June).

GERMANFEST

NE – Fort Wayne. Headwaters Park Festival Center. www.germanfest.org . German heritage celebrated with folk music, dancing, food, kindertag, sports, exhibitions. Admission. (second week of June)

INDIANAPOLIS SCOTTISH HIGHLAND GAMES & FESTIVAL

C – Indianapolis https://www.facebook.com/IndyScotGamesAndFest/ Sheep herding, bagpipes, Scottish dancing and food, competitions. FREE. (second Saturday in June)

GREEK FESTIVAL

NE – Fort Wayne. Headwaters Park. www.fortwaynegreekfestival.org Greek food, music, dancing and art. Admission. (last weekend in June)

JULY

JULY 4ᵀᴴ CELEBRATIONS

Live entertainment, parade, carnival, food, fireworks.

- ❑ **C – Fishers**. A Glorious Fourth. Conner Prairie. (317) 776-6000 or www.connerprairie.org . Reading of the Declaration of Independence. Admission.
- ❑ **C – Indianapolis**. Fourth Fest. Downtown (317) 633-6363. Free
- ❑ **C – Indianapolis**. Ice Cream Social. President Benjamin Harrison's Home. (317) 631-1898. Period costumed characters roam the grounds and talk to you. Admission.
- ❑ **CE – Metamora**. Old Fashioned 4ᵗʰ of July. Main Street. (765) 647-2109. FREE.
- ❑ **CW – Lafayette, West Lafayette**. Downtown and 9ᵗʰ Street Hill Historic district. (800) 872-6648. Flag parade, cannon firings.
- ❑ **NC – Elkhart**. Sky Concert. (800) 377-3579.
- ❑ **NE – Geneva**, Amishville USA. (260) 589-3536.
- ❑ **NE – Huntington**. Forks of Wabash. (260) 356-1903.
- ❑ **NW – Crown Point**. www.cpjuly4.com . Doll and pet parade.
- ❑ **NW – LaPorte**. Jaycees' 4ᵗʰ of July. (219) 324-5392. Over 50 years with fly over of military jets. Admission. Weeklong.
- ❑ **NW – Wolcott**. Wolcott House Grounds. (219) 279-2123. FREE. (July 3ʳᵈ & 4ᵗʰ)
- ❑ **SE – Corydon**. Old Settlers Day. Old Capitol Square. (812) 738-4890. Pioneer demonstrations. No Admission.
- ❑ **SW – Evansville**. Freedom Festival. Downtown riverfront. www.evansvillefreedomfestival.org . Thunder on the Ohio, Thunder Air, Hot Air Balloons. Admission. (five day event)

SCOTTISH FESTIVAL

C – Columbus. Mill Race Park. www.scottishfestival.org Bagpipe bands, sheepdog trials, Highland dancing, athletic competitions and traditional foods. Admission. (third weekend in July)

HOT DOG FESTIVAL

C – **Frankfort**. Courthouse Square. https://www.facebook.com/FrankfortHotDogFestival/ Hot dogs with every topping imaginable! Puppy Park with children's activities and other "dog" related events. FREE. (last weekend in July)

ELKHART COUNTY 4-H FAIR

NC – **Goshen**, County Fairgrounds. www.4hfair.org .One of the largest county fairs in the nation with 4-H exhibits, demos, food, carnival and free top-name entertainment. Admission. (July)

HAYNES-APPERSON FESTIVAL

NC – **Kokomo**. Downtown. http://haynesappersonfestival.org/. The town celebrates its automotive history with Haynes Museum tours, car shows, a parade, carnival, food, and talent contest. FREE. (first weekend in July)

CIRCUS CITY FESTIVAL

NC – **Peru**. Circus City Festival Arena. www.perucircus.com . Best amateur youth performances include flying trapeze, high wire, bareback riding. Carnival downtown. Tour Hall of Fame, rides, food. Admission. (third week of July)

SWISS DAYS

NE – **Berne**. Downtown. https://swissdaysberne.com/ Yodeling, folk dancing, concerts, cheese making factory tours, Swiss food and famous apple dumplings. FREE. (last weekend in July)

THREE RIVERS FESTIVAL

NE – **Fort Wayne**. Headwaters Park. www.threeriversfestival.org . Children's Fest, McDonald's Parade, music, raft race, fireworks. Admission to some events. (mid-month, weeklong in July)

GREAT MILL RACE

NW – **Cutler**. Adam's Mill. (765) 463-7893. Boat races every half hour; crafts, displays, mill tours and demonstrations, food. FREE. (second Saturday in July)

PIEROGI FESTIVAL

NW – Whiting. Historic Downtown. http://pierogifest.net/ Slovak and Polish delicacies, music, dancing, parade. FREE. (last weekend in July)

MADISON REGATTA

SE – Madison. Ohio River. www.madisonregatta.com . Races featuring the world's fastest boats-unlimited hydroplanes. Also balloon race, parade, music, fireworks. Some events have admission. (July 4th week)

LIMESTONE HERITAGE FESTIVAL

SW   –   Bedford.   Brian   Lane   Way. www.facebook.com/limestoneheritagefestival. An important Indiana resource, Bedford stone was used to build the Empire State Building and the Pentagon.   Quarry tours, parade, fireworks, sculpture exhibits and competition. No Admission. (week up to July 4th)

AUGUST

GLASS FESTIVAL

C – Elwood. Callaway Park. http://elwoodglassfestival.com   Glass factory tours include: Prestige Art Glass, SR 13 (765) 552-0688; Spencers Lapidary (marbles), SR 37 & SR 13 (765) 552-0784; The House of Glass, SR 28 (765) 552-6841. Food, carnival, volksmarch, parade. FREE. (third weekend in August)

INDIANA STATE FAIR

C – Indianapolis. State Fairgrounds. https://www.indianastatefair.com/ Indiana's best exhibitors, competitors and entertainers are joined by top national entertainment. Blue ribbon agricultural exhibits, top Indiana youth exhibitors. Hours 6:00am to late evening. Admission. (middle of August for 11 days)

PICKLE FEST

NE – St. Joe. (State Route 1, off I-69 & Dupont) www.stjoepicklefestival.com . Start with a pickle factory tour. Pickle Derby, Pickle People Contest, variety of children's activities (including a large petting zoo), great entertainment, fireworks, and a huge craft tent. FREE. (second full weekend in August)

POTATO FEST

NW   –   **Medaryville.**   Downtown. https://www.facebook.com/groups/284109807748360/ Spuds with every imaginable topping, curly fries, numerous potato creations. FREE. (mid-month weekend in August)

DAN PATCH DAYS

NW – Oxford. Rommel Park. https://www.danpatchdays.org/   Rodeo, draft horse pull, Dan Patch memorabilia (famous pacer horse), parade, entertainment, bingo. Admission. (first weekend in August)

STRASSENFEST

SW – Jasper. Downtown. www.jasperstrassenfest.org . German heritage with music, food, talent show. Admission. (first weekend in August)

SCHWEIZER FEST

SW – Tell City, Hall Park. http://tellcityschweizerfest.com/   Swiss-German heritage celebration offering free entertainment, authentic food, rides and market. FREE. (second week in August)

WATERMELON FESTIVAL

SW   –   **Vincennes.**   Downtown. https://www.knoxcountychamber.com/watermelon-festival/   Free watermelon, food sidewalk sales, sports competition, games pageants, historic site tours. (first weekend in August)

SEPTEMBER

INDIAN POW-WOWS

A day to hear drums, smell fry bread, watch dancers, listen to tales, and visit tents of Native American traders. Traditional arts, clothing, language & history.

❑   **C – Anderson.** Andersontown PowWow and Indian Market. www.andersontownpowwow.org (weekend after Labor Day)

❏   **CW – Attica.** Potawatomi Festival. Wabash riverfront. Admission. (third weekend in September) https://www.facebook.com/pokagonband/
❏   **SW – Evansville**. Native American Days. Angel Mounds. FREE. (last weekend in September)

THE GREEK FESTIVAL

C – Indianapolis, Holy Trinity Greek Orthodox Church. www.indygreekfest.org has been an Indianapolis tradition for 31 years. Always the weekend after Labor Day. Come join us rain or shine for music, food and dancing. Enjoy traditional Greek music by the Bill Simons band, home made pastries, traditional Greek foods. Admission. (weekend after Labor Day)

OLD JAIL MUSEUM BREAKOUT

CW – Crawfordsville. Old Jail Museum. (800) 866-3973. See the only rotary jail built in Indiana (cells turn every half hour). Music, entertainment, children's events, free refreshments. FREE. (Labor Day)

FAIRMONT MUSEUM DAYS FESTIVAL

NC – Fairmount. Main Street. (765) 948-4555 or www.jamesdeanartifacts.com . Tour Fairmount Historical Museum/James Dean Museum. Parade, look-alike contest, entertainment with 50's music, dance contest, all James Dean movies playing, plus recognition of hometowner, Jim Davis' "Garfield" series. FREE. (last weekend in September)

BLUEBERRY FESTIVAL

NC – Plymouth. Marshall County. Centennial Park. (888) 936-5020 or www.blueberryfestival.org . Largest 3 day festival in Indiana with blueberry treats like milkshakes, pie and ice cream. Parade, circus, fireworks, fair food. FREE. (Labor Day Weekend)

AUBURN-CORD DUESENBERG FESTIVAL

NE – Auburn. (260) 925-3600 or www.acdfestival.org . Classic car showcase. Parade of Classics, automotive museums, entertainment and a kids art tent. Admission. (Labor Day Weekend)

MARSHMALLOW FESTIVAL

NE – Ligonier. Main Street. (260) 894-9000 or www.marshmallowfestival.com The country's center for marshmallow making. Bake-off, marshmallow putting contest, games, rides, entertainment, parade, area factory history. FREE. (Labor Day Weekend)

STEAM & POWER SHOW

NW – Hesston. Steam Museum. (219) 872-5055. www.hesston.org Rated Top 10 Festival. Steam train rides across 155 scenic acres. Also see restored steam power plant, sawmill, antique engines, tractors. Admission. (Labor Day Weekend)

BALLOONFEST

NW – Valparaiso. Porter county Fairgrounds. (219) 462-1209. 20 some balloons with launch and glows, food, souvenirs. Admission. (first weekend after Labor Day)

POPCORN FESTIVAL

NW – Valparaiso. Downtown. www.popcornfest.org In honor of the late Orville Redenbacher and his origin from this town. Popcorn parade, hot air balloon show, children's play areas, food, live entertainment. FREE. (first weekend after Labor Day)

FOSSIL FEST

SE – Clarksville. Falls of the Ohio State Park. (812) 280-9970. Special exhibits, guest speakers, fossil & mineral dealers, children's activity area and fossil collection piles donated by Liter's Quarry. (third weekend in September)

PUMPKIN SHOW

SE – Versailles. Courthouse Square. https://versaillespumpkinshow.com/ Carnival, concessions, contest, entertainment, parade. Giant pumpkin weighing & pumpkin foods. FREE. (last weekend in September)

PUMPKIN FESTIVAL

SW – French Lick. Downtown, Maple St & SR56. https://www.facebook.com/OCPumpkinFestival/ Big Pumpkin Parade, carnival, food. FREE. (last week in September to beginning of October)

SEPTEMBER / OCTOBER

HARVEST FESTIVALS

Horses plow fields, antique tractors, chuckwagon-style dinner, corn shredding, tractor pull, hayrides, corn shucking competition and straw baling.

- ❑ **C – Fishers**. Country Fair. Conner Prairie. (800) 966-1836. Admission. (third weekend in September)
- ❑ Admission. (Labor Day Weekend)
- ❑ **NW – Valparaiso**, Sunset Farm Hill County Park (US 6 & Meridian Road). (219) 465-3586.
- ❑ **NW – Wanatah**. Scarecrow Festival. US 421 & US 30. (219) 733-2183. FREE. (fourth weekend in September)

FALL PLAYLANDS

Corn Mazes, Hayrides, Petting Animals, Pick-a-Pumpkin patches, Scarecrows, Painted Pumpkins, Pumpkin Carving Contests, refreshments and entertainment. Admission.

- ❑ **C – Greenfield**. S&H Campground (2573 W 100 North), Family Pumpkin Patch and Poppin' Corn Maze. www.sandhcampground.com
- ❑ **C – Indianapolis**. Waterman's Farm Market. 7010 E. Raymond St. www.watermansfamilyfarm.com (October, daily)
- ❑ **C – Noblesville**. Stonycreek Farm. www.stonycreekfarm.net (early September-October)
- ❑ **CE – Cambridge City**. Dougherty Orchards. www.facebook.com/doughertyorchard Also, Apple House Tours. (September – December, Daily)
- ❑ **NC – Goshen**. Kercher's Sunrise Orchards. CR 38. www.kerchersorchard.com (Mid-September to Mid-October)
- ❑ **NC - Peru**. McClures Orchard www.mccluresorchard.com
- ❑ **NE - Ligonier**. Pumpkin Fantasyland. Fashion Farm, 1680 Lincolnway West .www.pumpkinfantasyland.com (October)
- ❑ **NW – Hobart**. County Line Orchard. www.countylineorchard.com (October)

For updates, visit our website: www.KidsLoveTravel.com

- ❏ **NW** – Wanatah Guse Christmas Tree Farm.
  www.gusechristmastrees.com
- ❏ **SE – Starlight**. Joe Huber Family Farm & Restaurant. 2421
  Scottsville Road (I – 64 East to Exit 119). (877) JOE HUBERS
  or www.huberwinery.com . Also apple orchard in September
  (wagon ride to orchard for picking). (September / October)

APPLE FESTIVALS

Apple peeling and pie-eating contests, apple foods demos, apple foods-
pies, donuts, cider, butter. Carnival.

- ❏ **C – Danville**. Heartland Apple Festival, Beasley's Orchard
  (Rockville Road just east of downtown Danville).
  www.beasleysorchard.com . Farming animal shows, puppets,
  storytelling. $5.00/vehicle. (first and second weekend in October)
- ❏ **C - Pendleton**. Grabow's Orchard. 6397 SR 13 off I-69.
  Raspberries too! www.graboworchard.com (last Saturday in
  September)
- ❏ **C – Sheridan**. Stuckey Farm Market, (2 ½ miles north of SR32
  on County Line Rd). www.stuckeyfarm.com FREE. (June-
  November, daily except Sunday)
- ❏ **NC - Nappanee**. www.amishacres.com (800) 517-9739. 600 lb.
  Apple pie. FREE. (third weekend in September)
- ❏ **NC – Peru**. McClure's Tate Orchard. (765) 985-2467 or
  www.mccluresorchard.com . Apples and dumplings.
- ❏ **NW – Laporte**. Garwood Orchards.
  www.facebook.com/garwoodappleorchard (mid-month
  Saturday in September)
- ❏ **SE – Batesville**. Liberty Park. (812) 933-3103. AppleFest,
  carriage rides. FREE. (last weekend in September)

OKTOBERFEST

German music and dance, food, parade, carnival and hayrides.

- ❑   **SW – Huntingburg**. Herbstfest. City Park at First & Cherry Streets. (812) 683-5699. (first long weekend in October)
- ❑   **SW– New Harmony**. Kunstfest. (800) 231-2168. Petting zoo, wagon rides, general store, historic homes to tour. FREE, some fees for historic tours. (two weekends after Labor Day)
- ❑   **CW – Terre Haute**. Wabash Valley Fairgrounds, US 41 South. (812) 466-2107. Admission (12+). (first two Saturdays in October)

OCTOBER

HOOSIER STORYTELLING FESTIVAL

C – Indianapolis. Indiana Museum and Military Park http://storytellingarts.org/ . Annual festival presenting national and regional storytellers performing on multiple stages. Children's Stage, Family Storytelling Activities Tent (crafts, activities and performances to enhance the storytelling experience), Sharing Hoosier History Through Stories, and A Story Cabaret. These tellers from around the country will share music and stories from their childhoods, cultures, and heritages. Admission. (first full week of October, Wednesday-Saturday)

PARKE COUNTY COVERED BRIDGE FESTIVAL

CW – Ten days in the middle of October. County celebrates Indiana's historic past with 32 Historic Covered Bridges. Hours: 9:00am-6:00pm. FREE. www.coveredbridges.com .

- ❑   **Rockville** – Headquarters. Sample cooking and crafts. Bus tours.
- ❑   **Billie Creek Village** – America's largest gathering of turn-of-the-century craftsmen. 3 bridges, entertainment, horse-pulled wagon rides, authentic foods and costumes. Admission. BLACK ROUTE.
- ❑   **Bridgeton** – 245-foot double-span covered bridge above the dam, waterfall near a working gristmill. Weaver, crafters, food. RED ROUTE.

❑ **Mansfield** – Historic Village, 1820's water-powered grist mill, 1867 covered bridge. BLACK ROUTE.

❑ **Mecca** – 2 historic schoolhouses, covered bridge, 1800's outdoor metal jail, old clay tile factory, crafts, foods, and dancing on the bridge. BROWN ROUTE & RED ROUTE.

❑ **Montezuma** – Historic river town and home of the Wabash-Erie Canal bed, Aztec trading post, hog roast, hayrides, trail rides.

❑ **Rosedale** – Potato fields, antique equipment. RED ROUTE.

❑ **Tangier** – 5 covered bridges, serve Tangier's famous "buried roast beef". BLUE & YELLOW ROUTE.

LEWIS AND CLARK RIVER FESTIVAL

SE – **Clarksville**, Falls of the Ohio State Park, George Rogers Clark Homesite. www.fallsoftheohio.org . (812) 283-4999. Re-enactors portray William Clark, Meriwether Lewis and George Rogers Clark, and the Lewis and Clark "Corps of Discovery" expedition. They left Mill Creek in Clarksville in 1803 to discover the West. Children's games, craft demos and book signings. (last weekend in October)

NOVEMBER

INTERNATIONAL FESTIVAL

C – **Indianapolis**, West Pavilion, Indiana State Fairgrounds. (317) 236-6515 or www.indyinternationalfestival.org . Hosted by The Nationalities Council of Indiana. Event features cultural displays, artist demonstrations, entertainment, ethnic foods, and a global bazaar. Admission. (first long weekend in November)

NOVEMBER / DECEMBER

CHRISTMAS EXPRESS

CE– **Connersville**.   Whitewater   Valley   Railroad. www.whitewatervalleyrr.org . Special holiday shopping excursions to Metamora. Santa Claus rides these trains to add to the holiday fun. Early reservations highly recommended. Admission (Friday nights, Saturday & Sunday afternoons for the three weekends following Thanksgiving)

FESTIVAL OF GINGERBREAD

NE – Fort Wayne. Old City Hall Historical Museum. (260) 426-2882. Creations of fantasy gingerbread houses on display. (Children's to Professional categories) FREE. (Thanksgiving through mid-December)

FESTIVAL OF LIGHTS

Lighted roadways or walkways. Entertainment. Carolers. Santa. Themed with characters and historical events. (Evenings beginning the weekend of Thanksgiving through December unless noted otherwise)

- ❑ **C – Columbus**. Mill Race Park. (800) 468-6564 or www.columbus.in.us . Over 2 million lights. Small Admission.
- ❑ **C – Fishers**. Conner Prairie by Candlelight. (800) 966-1836 or www.connerprairie.org . Walk-thru a holiday village 1836 and Festival of Gingerbread display. Admission/Reservations. (December, Wednesday-Sunday evenings)
- ❑ **C – Indianapolis**. Christmas at the Zoo. Indianapolis Zoo. (317) 630-2001. 700,000 lights and 180 displays. Train & Trolley Rides. Admission.
- ❑ **CE – Metamora**. Old Fashioned Christmas Walk. (765) 647-6512 or www.emetamora.com . Live nativity. Luminaries along roads and canal banks. FREE.
- ❑ **CE – Muncie**. Minnetrista Cultural Center & Gardens. (765) 282-4848 or www.mccoak.org . Luminaria Walk.
- ❑ **NC – Marion**. Christmas City Walkway of Lights, Riverwalk. (800) 662-9474 or www.walkwayoflights.com . Walk or drive, Gift shop. Daily. FREE.
- ❑ **NW – Valparaiso**. Holiday Lights. Sunset Hill Farm County Park, Hwy. 6. (219) 465-3586. (Thanksgiving thru first weekend in December)
- ❑ **SE – Rising Sun**. Holiday Winter Walk. Riverfront. Turn of the century light display on the riverfront, Santa's Castle and horse-drawn carriage. FREE. (first weekend in December)
- ❑ **SW – Evansville**. Fantasy of Lights. Garvin Park. (812)474-2348. Admission.
- ❑ **SW – Santa Claus**. (812) 937-2848. Tour thru Christmas Lake Village.

DECEMBER

HOLIDAY OPEN HOUSES

Holiday decorated historic homes with costumed interpreters and special music and refreshments.

- ❑ **C – Anderson**. Gruenewalt House. (765) 646-5771. (first weekend in December)
- ❑ **C – Indianapolis**. President Benjamin Harrison Home. (317) 631-1888. Family Christmas - meet President Harrison and the household staff in various rooms through the house. Admission. (weekends from Thanksgiving through December)
- ❑ **CE – Cambridge City**. Family Christmas Festival at Huddleston Farmhouse Inn. (765) 478-3172. (Early to mid-December)
- ❑ **CE – Richmond**. Christmas at Wayne County Museum. (765) 962-5756. (first Sunday in December)
- ❑ **CW – Lafayette**. Victorian Christmas Tour of Fowler House, Tippecanoe County Museum. (765) 476-8402 or **www.tcha.mus.in.us**
- ❑ **NC – Bristol**. A Victorian Christmas Celebration. Elkhart County Museum. (574) 848-4322. Many Victorian Christmas characters and meal. Admission. (first or second weekend in December)
- ❑ **NC– Elkhart**. Ruthmere Museum. (800) 517-9737. (first Saturday in December)
- ❑ **NC – Kokomo**. Christmas at the Seiberling Mansion. (765) 452-4314. Admission. (Thanksgiving weekend to third week of December)
- ❑ **NC – South Bend**. Christmas at Copshaholm. (574) 235-9664. Admission. (Thanksgiving weekend to week after New Years)
- ❑ **NE – Geneva**. Limberlost State Historic Site. (260) 368-7428. (second weekend in December)
- ❑ **NE – Huntington**. Christmas at the Forks. (260) 356-1903. (first weekend in December)
- ❑ **NE – Rome City**. Gene-Stratton Porter Home. (260) 854-3790. (second weekend in November)

❑ **NW – Lowell**. Christmas at Buckley Homestead. (219) 696-6769. (first weekend in December)

❑ **NW – Michigan City**. Christmas at Barker Mansion, 631 Washington St. Admission. (first Saturday in December to mid-January)

❑ **NW – Porter**. Christmas in the Dunes. Chellberg Farm & Bailly Homestead. (219) 926-7561. (second Sunday in December)

❑ **SE – Aurora**. Hillforest Mansion, 213 Fifth St.. (812) 926-0087 or **www.dearborncounty.org**. Victorian Christmas. Admission. (first two weekends in December)

❑ **SE – Vevay**. Over the River and Through the Woods, Downtown. Admission. (first weekend in December)

❑ **SW – Evansville**. Rietz Home. (812) 426-1871. (Thanksgiving week to Christmas week, daily except Monday)

❑ **SW – Gentryville**. Christmas through the Ages at Col. William Jones State Historic Site. (812) 937-2802. (second weekend in December)

❑ **SW – New Harmony**. (812) 682-4488. Historic homes / village and museum. Admission. (first Saturday in December)

CIRCLE OF LIGHTS

C – Indianapolis. Monument Circle. https://downtownindy.org/events/circle-of-lights Lighting of the "World's Largest Christmas Tree" plus singing from the Indianapolis Children's Choir. FREE. (December, mid-month thru first week of January)

POLAR BEAR EXPRESS

C – Noblesville. Nickel Plate Rail. Train tickets include a reading and visual presentation of the popular story "The Polar Express", train ride and snacks. Admission and reservations. (December, first two weekends)

CHRISTMAS WALK IN THE PARK

CW – Terre Haute. Fowler Park Pioneer Log Village & Deming Park. https://terrehilldays.com/christmas-in-the-park/ Historic village streets and shelters decorated for the holidays, dulcimer music, refreshments. Dress warmly, bring a flashlight. Ride old-fashioned carriages or mini-trains. FREE. (Thanksgiving weekend and first weekend in December)

LIVE NATIVITY SCENE

NE – Shipshewana. Downtown. www.shipshewana.com . (260) 768-4163 or Costumed interpreters re-enact and celebrate the birth of Christ. Live animals and caroling too. FREE. (second weekend in December)

SANTA CANDY CANE EXPRESS

NW – Hesston Steam Museum. (219) 872-5055 or www.hesston.org . Visit with Santa in his caboose and take a cozy winter train ride in the first class enclosed coach. FREE (first two weekends in December)

HOLLYDAZE

SW – Evansville. Mesker Park Zoo. www.meskerparkzoo.com . Meet zoo critters, create tasty treats for animals, make a take-home craft, and meet Santa and Mrs. Claus. Free drinks and cookies served. Admission. (second weekend in December)

SANTA CLAUS POST OFFICE

SW – Santa Claus. Hwy 162 and 245. (812) 937-4469. Nation's only post office with a "Santa Claus" postmark – 45 N Kringle Place, 47579 (daily except Sunday in December)

NEW YEAR'S EVE CELEBRATION

Non-alcoholic party includes music, dance, clowns, storytellers, magicians, juggling and fireworks.

❑   **C – Indianapolis.** Indiana State Museum (day) or Indianapolis Zoo (evening) (317) 232-1637. Admission

❑   **NC – Elkhart.** FamilyFest. (800) 262-8161. Admission.

❑   **SW – Evansville.** First Night. (812) 422-2111. Admission.

YEAR LONG

PIONEER DAYS / ENCAMPMENTS

Early 1800's frontier life. Period costumed townsfolk, soldiers, Native Americans. See fur trading posts, kids' infantry, barber shop medicine, and old-fashioned games. Demonstrations of spinning, broom making, dancing, weaving, woodcarving, blacksmiths and tomahawk throwing. Open hearth cooking with period foods for sale like kettle popcorn and chips, cider, stew, barbecue, buffalo burgers, dumplings, apple butter, ham & beans, birch tea and Indian fry bread.

APRIL

MOUNTAIN MEN RENDEZVOUS

CW – Bridgeton. www.coveredbridges.com . (765) 548-2136. Located around Parke counties oldest home...the 1822 Case Log Cabin. See the mill in operation (est. 1823) and stroll through the camps. FREE. (last weekend in April)

REDBUD TRAIL RENDEZVOUS

NC–Rochester.   www.facebook.com/red.bud.trail.rendezvous.20/ Fulton County Historical Society Grounds. (574) 223-4436. Admission. (April)

MAY

MORGAN'S RAID, SCOTT COUNTY

SE – Lexington, Township Park. (812) 752-7270 Admission. (Memorial Day weekend).

SPIRIT OF VINCENNES RENDEZVOUS

SW – Vincennes. French Commons. (812) 886-6443 or www.spiritofvincennes.org . Battlefield activities of George Rogers Clark. Admission. (Memorial Day weekend)

AUGUST

STEAM & GAS SHOW

CW – Perrysville. Skinner Farm Museum & Village. SR32W http://skinnervillage.eshire.net/ Admission (third weekend in August)

For updates, visit our website: www.KidsLoveTravel.com

SEPTEMBER

TRAIL OF COURAGE LIVING HISTORY FESTIVAL

NC – Rochester, FCHS grounds four miles north of Rochester on US 31. https://www.facebook.com/Trailofcouragelvinghistoryfestival/ The Trail of Courage portrays history when northern Indiana was still Potawatomi territory, before the terrible forced removal of 1838, known as the Trail of Death. Each year the festival honors a different Potawatomi family that had ancestors on the Trail of Death or signed treaties in Indiana. The public is invited to join in Indian dances from 2 to 4 p.m., held in an arena encircled by teepees. This program of Indian dances is an educational exhibit, not a Pow Wow. There is also a recreation of Chippeway, the first trading post, post office and village in Fulton County in 1832. Canoe rides; muzzle loading shooting and tomahawk throwing contests, and a frontier blab school adds to the frontier activities. Admission. (third weekend in Sept)

JOHNNY APPLESEED FESTIVAL

NE – Fort Wayne. Johnny Appleseed Park. www.johnnyappleseedfest.com Celebrate the life and times of John Chapman. 100,000 attendance. Vendors and musicians wear period dress. FREE. (third weekend in September)

FORKS OF THE WABASH PIONEER FESTIVAL

NE – Huntington. Hiers Park. https://pioneerfestival.org/ Admission. (third or fourth weekend in September)

STONE'S TRACE PIONEER FESTIVAL

NE – Ligonier. (888) 417-3562 or www.stonestrace.com Pony cart rides, tour of Stone's Tavern, pioneer music, tomahawk throwing, circuit riding preacher, women's skillet throw, log splitting, primitive muzzle loading demos, food and entertainment. Admission. (wknd after Labor Day)

BUCKSKINNERS RENDEZVOUS

NW - **Cutler**.Adams Mill. https://www.visitmuscatine.com/156/Buckskinners-Rendezvous FREE. (last Saturday in Saturday)

DUNELAND HARVEST FESTIVAL

NW – Porter. Chellberg Farm & Bailly Homestead. https://www.nps.gov/indu/learn/news/duneland-fall-festival-at-the-national-park.htm FREE. (third weekend in September)

OLD SETTLERS DAYS

SE – Salem. John Hays Center. https://www.facebook.com/osdwashingtoncounty/ Storytelling, pioneer kids activities. FREE. (mid-month in September)

OCTOBER

CIVIL WAR DAYS & LIVING HISTORY

CE – Hartford City. SR 26E. www.hartfordcitycwdays.com . (765) 348-4319. Also tour a medical training school. Admission. (second weekend in Oct)

CANAL DAYS & TRADERS RENDEZVOUS

CE – Metamora. (765) 647-2194 or www.metamora.com . Little shops plus historical vendors and re-enactors. FREE. (first weekend in October)

PIONEER DAYS

CW – Terre Haute. Fowler Park Grist Mill area. (812) 462-3391. FREE. (first weekend in October)

FEAST OF THE HUNTER'S MOON

CW – West Lafayette. Fort Quiatenon Historic Park. South River Road. http://feastofthehuntersmoon.org Re-creation of life at this 18th century French trading post. Admission. (first weekend in Oct)

MISSISSINEWA 1812

NC – Marion. Battlefield. https://www.mississinewa1812.com/ Largest War of 1812 living history event in the U.S. with average attendance of 30,000. Admission. (end of first full week of October)

APPLE FESTIVAL

NE – Kendallville, Noble County Fairgrounds. (260) 347-4035 or www.kendallvilleapplefestival.com . Pioneer festival highlights the years 1800-1865. Skill demonstrators, primitive area, entertainment, kid's activities, antiques, crafts, and foods. FREE. (first weekend in October)

THE ARTS

TOURS